Sally Morgan was born in Perth, Western Australia, in 1951. She completed a Bachelor of Arts degree at The University of Western Australia in 1974. She also has post-graduate diplomas from The Western Australian Institute of Technology (now Curtin University of Technology) in Counselling Psychology and Computing and Library Studies. She is married with three children.

As well as writing, Sally Morgan has also established a national reputation as an artist. She has works in numerous private and public collections both in Australia and North America. Her first book, *My Place*, became and instant national best-seller, and has been published to considerable acclaim in Britain and North America. *Wanamurraganya: The Story of Jack McPhee* is her second book.

Sally's Story

Sally's Story

SALLY MORGAN

edited by Barbara Ker Wilson

FREMANTLE ARTS CENTRE PRESS

First published 1990 by
FREMANTLE ARTS CENTRE PRESS
1 Finnerty Street (PO Box 891), Fremantle
Western Australia, 6160.

Original unabridged edition of *My Place* published 1987.

Editor Barbara Ker Wilson.
Designed by John Douglass.
Production Manager Helen Idle.

Typeset in 11/12pt Clearface by Typestyle, Perth, Western Australia
and printed on 100gsm Woodfree by Tien Wah Press (Pte.) Ltd,
Singapore.

National Library of Australia
Cataloguing-in-publication data

Morgan, Sally, 1951-
    Sally's story.

    ISBN 0 949206 78 4.

    1. Morgan, Sally, 1951 -   . [2]. Aborigines, Australian
    - Biography - Juvenile literature. [3]. Aborigines,
    Australian - Women - Biography - Juvenile literature.
    [4]. Aborigines, Australian - Social life and customs -
    Juvenile literature. I. Wilson, Barbara Ker, 1929-
    II. Morgan, Sally, 1951-   . My Place. III Title.
    IV. Title: My Place.

994.00499 15

To My Family

How deprived we would have been
if we had been willing
to let things stay as they were.
We would have survived,
but not as a whole people.
We would never have known
our place.

ACKNOWLEDGEMENTS

Fremantle Arts Centre Press receives financial assistance from the Western Australian Department for the Arts.

Some of the personal names included in this book have been changed, or only first names included, to protect the privacy of those concerned.

CONTENTS

1

THE HOSPITAL

The hospital again, and the echo of my reluctant feet through the long, empty corridors. I hated hospitals and hospital smells. I hated the bare boards that gleamed with polish, and the flashes of shiny chrome that snatched my distorted shape as we hurried past. I was a grubby five-year-old in an alien environment.

Sometimes, I hated Dad for being sick and Mum for making me visit him. Mum only occasionally brought my younger sister and brother, Jill and Billy. I was always in the jockey's seat. My presence ensured no arguments. Mum was sick and tired of arguments.

We reached the end of the final corridor. The Doors were waiting for me again. Big, chunky doors covered in green linoleum. The linoleum had a swirl of white and the pattern reminded me of one of Mum's special rainbow cakes, cream with a swirl of pink and chocolate. I thought they were magic. There was no magic in The Doors: I knew what was behind them.

Sometimes, I pretended Dad wasn't really sick. I imagined that I'd walk through The Doors and he'd be smiling at me. 'Of course I'm not sick,' he'd say. 'Come and sit on my lap and talk to me.' And Mum would be there, laughing, and all of us would be happy.

Our entry into the ward never failed as a major event. The men there had few visitors. We were as important as the Red Cross lady who came around selling lollies and magazines.

'Well, *look* who's here,' they called.

'I think she's gotten taller, what d' ya reckon, Tom?'

'Fancy seeing you again, little girl.' I knew they weren't really surprised to see me; it was just a game they played.

After such an enthusiastic welcome, Mum would prompt me to talk. 'Say hello, darling,' she encouraged as she gave me a quick dig in the back. My silences were embarrassing to Mum. She usually told everyone I was shy. Actually, I was more scared than shy. I felt if I said anything at all, I'd just fall apart. There'd be me, in pieces on the floor. I was full of secret fears.

The men on the ward didn't give up easily. They continued their banter in the hope of winning me over.

'Come on sweetie, come over here and talk to me,' one old man coaxed as he held out a toffee. My feet were glued to the floor. I couldn't have moved even if I'd wanted to. This man reminded me of a ghost. His close-cropped hair stood straight up, like toothbrush nylon. His right leg was missing below the knee, and his loose skin reminded me of a plucked chicken. He tried to encourage me closer by leaning forward and holding out two Fantails. I waited for him to fall out of bed; I was sure he would if he leant any farther.

I kept telling myself he wasn't really a ghost, just an Old Soldier. Mum had confided that all these men were Old Soldiers. She lowered her voice when she told me. She had a fondness for them I didn't understand. I often wondered why Old Soldiers were so special. All of these men were missing arms or legs. Dad was the only one who was all there.

I tried not to look directly at any of them; I knew it was rude to stare. Once, I sat puzzling over a pair of wooden crutches for ages, trying to imagine what it would be like being lopsided. Could I get by with only one of my monkey legs or arms? That's what I called them. They weren't hairy, but they were long and skinny.

The Old Soldier rocked back on his pillow and I sneaked a quick glance at Dad. He was standing in his usual spot, by the side of his bed. He never came forward to greet us or called out, yet we belonged to him. His dressing-gown hung so loosely around his lanky body that he reminded me of the wire coat-hangers in our hall cupboard. Just a frame, that was Dad. The heart had gone out of him years ago.

Once Mum finished having a little talk and joke with the men, we moved over to Dad's bed and then out onto the hospital verandah.

The verandahs were the nicest place to sit; there were tables and chairs and you could look over the garden. Unfortunately, it took only a few minutes for the chairs to become uncomfortable. They were iron-framed, and tacked onto the seat and across the back were single jarrah slats painted all colours of the rainbow. When I was really bored, I entertained myself by mentally rearranging the colours so that they harmonised.

As Mum and Dad talked, I sniffed the air. It was a clear, blue spring day. I could smell the damp grass and feel the coolness of the breeze. It was such an optimistically beautiful day I felt like crying. Spring was always an emotional experience for me. It was for Nan, too. Only yesterday, she'd awakened me early to view her latest discovery. I had been in a deep sleep, but somehow her voice penetrated my dreams.

'Sally...wake up...' Even as I dreamt, I wondered where that voice was coming from. Faint, yet persistent, like the glow of a torch on a misty night. I didn't want to wake up. I burrowed deeper under the mound of coats and blankets piled on top of me. Sometimes, I thought coldness and thinness went together, because I was both.

Every night I'd call out, 'Mum...I'm cold.' And then, to speed her up, *'Mum...I'm freezing!'*

'Sally, you can't possibly be.' It was often her third trip to my bedside. She'd lift up the coat I'd pulled over my head and say, 'If I put any more on you, you'll suffocate. The others don't want all these coats on them.' I shared a bed with my brother Billy and my sister Jill. They never felt the cold.

I'd crane my head over the moulting fox-fur collar that trimmed one of the coats and retort, 'I'd rather suffocate than freeze!'

Now, sitting on the hospital verandah, I smiled as I remembered the way Nan had rocked my sleepy body back and forth to wake me up. I finally came up for air and murmured dopily, 'What is it? It's so early, Nan, do ya have to wake me so early?'

'Ssh, you'll wake the others. Don't you remember, I said I'd wake you early so you could hear the bullfrog again, and the bird?'

The bullfrog and the bird: how could I have forgotten? For the whole week Dad had been in hospital, she'd talked of nothing else.

With sudden decision I leapt from my bed and shivered my body into an old red jumper. Then, barefoot, I followed Nan out onto the back verandah.

'Sit still on the steps,' she told me. 'And be very quiet.' I was used to such warnings. I knew you never heard anything special unless you were very quiet. I pulled my hands up inside my sleeves for warmth, wrapped my arms around my legs, and waited.

The early morning was Nan's favourite time, when she always made some new discovery in the garden. A fat bobtail goanna, snake tracks, crickets with unusual feelers, myriads of creatures who had, for their own unique reasons, chosen our particular yard to reside in.

I wanted spring to last for ever, but it never did. Summer would come soon and the grass would yellow; even the carefully nurtured hospital grass wouldn't look as green. And the giant nasturtiums that crowded along our side fence and under our lemon tree would disappear. I wouldn't hunt for fairies any more, and Nan wouldn't wake me so early or so often.

I'd heard the bullfrog yesterday, it was one of Nan's

favourite creatures. She dug up a smaller, motley brown frog as well, and, after I inspected it, she buried it back safe in the earth. I shivered in the early morning breeze. I expected the bullfrog to be out again this morning. I gazed at the patch of dark earth where I'd last seen him. He'll come out any minute, I thought.

I felt excited. This morning, I was waiting for the bird call. Nan called it her special bird. Nobody had heard it but her. This morning, I was going to hear it, too.

'Broak, Broak!' The noise startled me. I smiled. That was the old bullfrog telling us he was broke again. I looked up at the sky, a cool, hazy blue with the promise of coming warmth.

Still no bird. I squirmed impatiently. Nan poked her stick in the dirt and said, 'It'll be here soon.' She spoke with certainty.

Suddenly, the yard filled with a high trilling sound. My eyes searched the trees. I couldn't see that bird, but his call was there. The music stopped as abruptly as it had begun.

Nan smiled at me. 'Did you hear him? Did you hear the bird call?'

'I heard him, Nan,' I whispered in awe.

What a magical moment it had been. I sighed. I was with Dad now, and there was no room for magic in hospitals. I peered at Mum and Dad. They both seemed nervous. I wondered how long I'd been day-dreaming.

Mum reached over and patted Dad's arm. 'How are you feeling, dear?'

'How do ya think!' It was a stupid question; he never got any better.

Pelican shoulders, I thought, as I watched him hunch forward in his chair. The tops of his shoulders poked up just like a pelican's. His fingers began to curl around the arms of his chair. He had slim hands for a man. I remembered someone saying once, 'Your father's a clever lad.' Was that where I got my ability to draw? I'd never seen Dad draw or paint, but I'd seen a letter he'd written once, it was beautiful. I knew he'd have trouble writing anything now, because his hands never stopped shaking. Sometimes I even had to light his cigarettes for him.

My gaze moved from his hands to his face. It dawned on me then that he'd lost more weight, and the realisation set my heart beating quickly. Dad caught my gaze; he was paler and the hollows under his cheek-bones were more defined. Only his hazel eyes were the same, confused, watching me.

'I'm making you something,' he said nervously. 'I'll go and get it.' He disappeared into the ward and returned a few minutes later with a small blue leather shoulder-bag. There was maroon thonging all the way around, except for the last part of the strap, which wasn't quite finished. As he laid it quietly in my lap, Mum said brightly, 'Isn't Daddy clever to make that for you?'

I stared at the bag. I was trapped. I mumbled a reluctant 'yes'. I wanted to run and fling myself on the grass. I wanted to bury my face so Dad couldn't see. I wanted to shout, 'No! I don't think Daddy's clever. *Anyone* could have made this bag. *He* doesn't think it's clever, either!'

By the time I looked up, Mum and Dad were both looking into the distance.

'Can we go now, Mummy?' I started guiltily. Had I really said that? My eyes widened as I waited for their reaction. Then I noticed that they weren't even looking at me. I breathed a slow sigh of relief. The last time I had voiced that question out loud, Mum had been cross and embarrassed, Dad silent. He was silent now. Such sad, sad eyes.

The visitors' bell rang unexpectedly. I wanted to leap up. Instead, I forced myself to sit still. I knew Mum wouldn't like it if I appeared too eager. Finally, Mum rose, and while she gave Dad a cheery goodbye, I slowly prised myself from my chair. The backs of my legs must have looked like a cross-walk, I could feel the indentations the hard slats had made in my skin.

As we walked into the ward, the men called out: 'What? Leaving already?'

'You weren't here for long, little girl.'

The Old Soldier with the Fantails smiled, and just as we

passed through The Doors and into the empty corridor, a voice called, 'We'll be waiting for you next time, little girl.'

Strong, cool air blew through the window all the way home in the bus. I kept thinking, can a person be wrinkled inside? I had never heard adults talk about such a thing, but that's how I felt, as though my insides needed ironing. I pushed my face into the wind and felt it roar up my nostrils and down into my throat. With cold ruthlessness it sought out my inside wrinkles, and flung them onto the passing road. I closed my eyes, relaxed and breathed out. And then, in a flash, I saw Dad's face. Those sad, silent eyes. I hadn't fooled him. He'd known what I'd been thinking.

Dad came home for a while a couple of weeks after that, and then, in the following January, 1957, Mum turned up on the doorstep with another baby. Her fourth. I was really cross with her. She showed me the white bundle and said, 'Isn't that a wonderful birthday present, Sally, to have your own little brother born on the same day as you?' I was disgusted. Fancy getting that for your birthday. And I couldn't understand Dad's attitude at all. He actually seemed pleased David had arrived!

2

SCHOOL

Mum chattered cheerfully as she led me down the bitumen path, through the main entrance to the grey weatherboard buildings. One look and I was convinced that, like the Hospital, this was a place dedicated to taking the spirit out of life.

I was certain Mum would never leave me in such a dreadful place, so I sat patiently, waiting for her to take me home.

'Have you got your sandwich?' she asked nervously.

'Yeah.'

'And a clean hankie?'

I nodded.

Mum paused. Then, looking off into the distance, she said brightly, 'I'm sure you're going to love it here.'

Alarm bells. I knew that tone of voice, it was the one she always used whenever she spoke about Dad getting better.

'You're gunna leave me here, aren't ya?'

Mum smiled guiltily. 'You'll love it. Look at all the kids the same age as you. You'll make friends. All children have to go to school someday, that's the law. I couldn't keep you home even if I wanted to. Now don't be silly, Sally, I'll stay with you till the bell goes.'

'What bell?'

'Oh...they ring a bell when it's time for you to line up to go into your class. And later on, they ring a bell when it's time for you to leave.'

'So I'm gunna spend all day listenin' for bells?'

'Sally,' Mum reasoned in an exasperated kind of way, 'don't be like that. You'll learn here, and they'll teach you how to add up. You love stories, don't you? They'll tell you stories.'

Just then, a tall, middle-aged lady, with hair the colour and shape of macaroni, emerged from the first class-room in the block.

'May I have your attention please?' she said loudly. Everyone immediately stopped talking. 'My name is Miss Glazberg. The bell will be going shortly,' she informed the mothers, 'and when that happens I want you to instruct your children to line up on the bitumen playground. And I would appreciate it if the mothers would all move off quickly and quietly after the children have lined up. That way, I will have plenty of time to settle them down and get to know them.'

I glared at Mum.

'I'll come with you to the line,' she whispered.

The bell rang suddenly, loudly, terrifyingly. I clutched Mum's arm.

Slowly, she led me to where the other children were beginning to gather. She removed my hands from her arm but I grabbed onto the skirt of her dress. Some of the other mothers began moving off as instructed, waving as they went. One little boy in front of me started to cry. Suddenly, I wanted to cry too.

'Come now, we can't have this,' said Miss Glazberg as she freed Mum's dress from my clutches.

'I have to go now, dear,' Mum said desperately.

Miss Glazberg wrenched my fingers from around Mum's thigh. 'Say goodbye to your mother.' It was too late, Mum had turned and fled to the safety of the verandah.

'*Mum*,' I called as she mounted the last wooden step,

'*Mum!*'

She turned quickly and waved, falling badly on the top step as she did so. I had no sympathy for her wounded ankle, or for the tears in her eyes.

'*Mum!*' I screamed as she hobbled off. '*Come back!*'

Despite the urgings of Miss Glazberg to follow the rest of the children inside, I stood firmly rooted to the bitumen playground, screaming and clutching for security my plastic toilet-bag and a Vegemite sandwich.

By the beginning of second term at school, I was the best reader in my class. Reading opened up new horizons for me, but it also created a hunger that school couldn't satisfy. Miss Glazberg could see no reason for me to have a new book when the rest of the children in my class were still struggling with the old one. Every day I endured the same old adventures of Nip and Fluff, and every day I found my eyes drawn to the back of the class where a small library was kept.

I pestered Mum so much about my reading that she finally dug up the courage to ask my teacher if I could have a new book. I felt quite proud, I knew she hated approaching my teacher about anything.

'I'm sorry, darling,' Mum told me that night, 'your teacher said you'll be getting a new book in Grade Two.'

There weren't many books at our house, but there were plenty of old newspapers, and I started trying to read those. One day, I found Dad's plumbing manuals in a box in the laundry, but the words were too difficult.

Towards the end of second term, Miss Glazberg told us there was going to be a night when all the parents came to school and looked at our work. Then, instead of our usual sheets of butcher's paper, she passed out clean, white rectangles, flat on one side and shiny on the other. I gazed in awe at my paper; it was crying out for a beautiful picture.

'Now children, I want you all to do a picture of your mother and your father. Only the very best ones will be chosen for display on Parents' Night.'

There was no doubt in my mind that mine would be one

of the chosen few. With great concentration and determination, I pored over my page, crayoning and detailing my parents. I kept my arm over my work so no one could copy. Suddenly, a hand tapped my shoulder and Miss Glazberg said, 'Let me see yours, Sally.' I sat back in my chair.

'Ooh, goodness me!' she muttered as she patted her heart. 'Oh no, dear, not like that!'

Before I could stop her, she picked up my page and walked quickly to her desk. I watched in dismay as my mother and father disappeared with a scrunch into her personal bin. The children around me snickered. It hadn't occurred to me you were meant to draw them with clothes on.

By the beginning of third term, I had developed an active dislike of school. I was bored and lonely. Even though the other children talked to me, I found it difficult to respond.

Dad didn't seem to be very interested in my schooling, either. He never asked me how I was going or whether I had problems. In fact, the closest contact Dad had with my education was a brutal encounter with my black print pencil. I was sharpening the pencil for school, and, just when I was satisfied with its razor-sharp tip, Dad strolled in and bent down to sit on the arm of my chair. Without thinking, I stood my pencil pointy-end upwards. On contact, Dad leapt up in pain and swore loudly. As he swung around, I waited for him to belt me. To my utter surprise, all he could manage was to splutter, 'Go to your room!'

'Why on earth did you do it, Sally?' Mum asked. I didn't really know. Curiosity about cause and effect, I guess.

I was allowed certain privileges now I was at school. The best one was being allowed to stay up later than the others and share Dad's tea. He had a drinking mate with a boat, and if there was a good catch, crayfish came our way. Fleshy, white crayfish and tomato dipped in vinegar, that was Dad's favourite meal. It was a happy time then, crays and tomatoes, Dad and me.

I knew some of Dad's tastes were a legacy of the war. That particular one from the time Italian partisans had sheltered

21

him from the Germans. Dad had taught me to sing the Communist anthem in Italian. *The Internationale*. I thought I was very clever being able to sing in another language.

We had some good times, then. Some nights, Dad would hide chocolates in the deep pockets of his overalls and we were allowed to fish them out. He'd laugh and joke, and when he swore, we knew he didn't really mean it.

Dad slipped in and out of our lives. He was often in hospital, and the longest he was at home at one time was about three months. He would seem to be all right for a while, but would rapidly deteriorate. He stayed in his room, drinking heavily. Soon he was back in hospital again.

Dad was a plumber by trade. Every time he returned from hospital, he had to try to find another job. Mum provided the only steady income, with various part-time jobs, mostly cleaning.

When Dad was happy, I wished he'd never change. I wanted him to be like that for ever, but just when things seemed to be looking up, the war would intrude and overwhelm us. The war had never ended for Dad. He lived with it day and night. It was a strange thing, because he'd told me how important it was to be free. I knew Australia was a free country, but Dad wasn't free. There were things in his head that wouldn't go away. Sometimes, I had the impression that if he could have got up and run away from himself, he would have.

Part of the reason I was unhappy at school was probably because I was worrying about what was happening at home. Sometimes, I was so tired I just wanted to lay my head on my desk and sleep. I only slept well at night when Dad was in hospital; there were no arguments then. I kept a vigil when Mum and Dad argued; so did Nan. I made a secret pact with myself. Awake, I was my parents' guardian angel; asleep, my power was gone. I was worried that one night something terrible might happen and I wouldn't be awake to stop it.

The following year Jill started school; I felt sure I would not be so lonely with her there.

As we joined the small groups of children and parents walking to school that first morning, I watched Jill curiously. She seemed neither excited nor daunted by the prospect of being away from home. I put her calmness down to ignorance, and felt sure that, once our walk led us within sight of school, Jill would break down.

'Hasn't the school got a lovely garden, Jilly?' Mum commented as we approached the entrance.

'Yeah, we've got roses like that.'

I narrowed my eyes and looked at her; not a tear in sight. Oh well, I thought, wait till it's time for Mum to leave.

'What do I do now?' Jill asked as she trotted up the verandah.

'Aah, ya have to wait for the bell. That's your class down there. Go and sit with Mum on the step, she'll be with you till the bell goes, but she won't be here all day.' I scanned her face. Poor kid, I thought, it hasn't sunk in yet.

Jill walked back and plopped down on the verandah step. I watched as Mum smiled at her in exactly the same way she'd smiled at me the previous year. Jill grinned back. Mum had actually convinced her she was going to like school.

Within a few minutes, the bell was ringing loudly. Mum waved and began moving off. I was shocked when Jill calmly took her place in the queue that was forming at the front of her class.

Just before Mum disappeared completely from sight, I saw her cast an anxious glance towards the Grade One line. Now, Jill, now! I thought. It was the perfect moment. For some reason, Jill sensed my interest, and turned and waved happily to me. I groaned in despair. She was obviously dumber than I'd suspected. 'Mum's going now!' I called out, but she was too busy chatting to the boy in front of her to reply.

I watched with a mixture of envy and surprise as she continued talking to the other children. They were all strangers to her, and yet she seemed to fit in, somehow. I knew then that, when it came to school, Jill and I would never agree.

My day-dreaming was suddenly interrupted by a deep voice calling, 'You girl, you with the long plaits, come here and pay attention.' I'd been so busy watching Jill that I'd failed to notice my class-mates had also formed a line.

My new teacher began slowly walking down the line, carefully inspecting each of her forty charges. 'Don't slouch. Stomach in, chest out, chin up!' She tapped my chin lightly with her wooden ruler. I attempted to follow her instructions, leaning so far backwards I nearly fell over.

We moved quietly into class. Our teacher drew herself up to her full height and said, 'I...am Miss Roberts.' Apart from her pause after the word 'I', she spoke quickly and very, very clearly.

'Now children, I...am going to hand out some reading books. You will all remain as quiet as mice while *I*'m doing this.'

I smiled to myself. It wasn't going to be so terrible after all, my new book was on its way.

I waited expectantly as Miss Roberts walked first down one row and then another. By the time she finally reached my desk, I was brimming over with excitement. She placed my book on my desk, and I couldn't help groaning out loud. It seemed that Dick, Dora, Nip and Fluff had somehow managed to graduate to Grade Two. In a way, I felt sorry for them. None of them lived near a swamp, and there was no mention of wild birds, snakes or goannas. All they ever did was visit the toy shop and play ball with Nip. I resigned myself to another year of boredom.

'Has Miss Roberts ever been in the army, Mum?' I asked one afternoon.

'What a strange question, whatever makes you ask that?'

'Well, when we line up for school she won't let us in the class unless we're all straight and stiff. She pokes you in the stomach and says, "Stomach in, chest out, eyes forward." Dad told me they do that in the army.'

Mum laughed; it was obvious she thought I was exaggerating again. However, the following week, she confided to me that Miss Roberts had, indeed, been in the Women's army. One of the cleaners at the school had told her. I found this information very interesting. Dad often talked about the army. He'd been too much of a non-conformist to take naturally to army life. Now I understood how he'd felt. I didn't like being told what to do either.

From then on, whenever I marched into class, I would silently sing an old army ditty Dad had taught me:

> *I'm in the army now*
> *I went to milk a cow*
> *The cow let-off and I took off*
> *I'm out of the army now!*

Jill, Billy and I loved rude songs. We often marched around the yard singing that one. Billy beat on his old tin drum and Jill and I pretended to blow army trumpets. I could play reveille, too. By placing a piece of paper tightly over a comb and blowing on it, I could produce a high-pitched, farty sort of sound that I could manipulate into a recognisable tune. Reveille was my favourite.

Towards the end of first term, I had an encounter with Miss Roberts that wiped out any confidence I might have had for the rest of the year.

Our school seats had a heavy metal frame, with jarrah slats spaced across the seat and back. One day, after what seemed hours of holding my arm in the air trying to attract Miss Roberts' attention, I was unable to avoid wetting myself.

Miss Roberts, intent on marking our latest tests, had failed to notice my desperately flailing arm. But one of the clean, shiny-haired girls next to me began to chant quietly, 'You've wet ya pa-ants, you've wet ya pa-ants!'

'I have not,' I denied hotly, 'it's just water under my chair.'

By this time, most of the surrounding children were starting to giggle.

Miss Roberts raised her horn-rimmed eyes and said firmly, '*Quiet* please! I...have an announcement to make.'

We were very impressed with Miss Roberts' use of the

word 'I'. For the whole term, I had been convinced Miss Roberts was even more important than the headmistress.

'I...have finished marking your test papers.' Under Miss Roberts' reign, our weekly tests had assumed great importance. We all waited anxiously to hear who had missed the mark this time.

'I...must commend you all on your efforts. All, except Rrrodney.' She always rolled her R's when she said Rodney.

'Rrrodney,' she continued, 'how many times have *I* told you bottom is spelt b-o-t-t-o-m *not* b-u-m!'

Rodney grinned, and we all snickered. I had a grudging admiration for Rodney. He'd been spelling bottom like that for three weeks now. He was my kind of person.

'Now,' she said, 'where is Sally, hmmmn?' She peered around the class in an attempt to locate my nondescript brown face amongst a sea of thirty-nine knowing smiles. 'Oh, there you are, dear.' I had been cowering behind the girl in front of me.

'Sally has, for the *first* time this year, managed to complete her test correctly. In fact, this week she is the only one to have done so.' Pausing, she allowed time for the greatness of my achievement to sink in. Everyone knew what was coming next. 'Well, Sally. Come out to the front and hold up your book. I...can tell the class is anxious to see your work.'

Miss Roberts waited patiently as I rose carefully to my feet. I hurriedly twisted the wet part of my dress around as far as I could, holding it tightly bunched in my left hand. With my knees locked together, and my left elbow jutting out at an unusual angle behind my back, I jerked spasmodically forward. Fortunately, Miss Roberts was gazing at my test book.

'I...want you to hold this up to the class so they can all see it. Look how eager they are to see a test that has scored one hundred per cent!'

Clutching my book in my right hand, I leant as far from Miss Roberts as possible.

My misshapen body must have alerted her to the fact that something was wrong, because she snapped impatiently,

'Hold the book with two hands! And put your dress down, we are not interested in seeing your pants!'

A wave of giggling swept over the class. As I patted down the full skirt of my blue cotton dress, Miss Roberts' large, sensitive nostrils flared violently, and she snorted in disgust. 'You dirty, dirty girl.' She shoved me out of the door.

'You sit out there and dry off!'

I sat alone and damp on the hard jarrah bench.

My attitude towards school took an even more rapid down-hill turn after that incident. I felt different from the other children in my class. They were the spick-and-span brigade. I was the grubby offender.

3

PICNIC

Things at home weren't getting any better. Dad had stopped even trying to get work, and was in hospital more than he was at home. He still lived in his favourite blue overalls, but he never hid chocolates in the pockets any more. He only hid himself, now. When he was home, he never came out of his room. The only thing he seemed interested in was the pub.

Our local pub was called the Raffles; it was situated on the banks of the Swan River. There was a group of returned soldiers who drank there. Give Dad a few beers down the Raffles with his mates and he was soon in another world. He forgot about us and Mum, and became one of the boys.

We kids often went to the pub with Dad. While he enjoyed himself in the bar, we sat, bored and forgotten, in the car. Summer was worst. Dad always wound the windows up in case anyone should try to steal us. He forbade us ever to get out. These precautions meant that on hot summer nights we nearly suffocated.

One summer's evening, I could stand it no longer. Dad had been gone for ages, and I'd given up all hope of him returning with some bags of potato chips. Somehow, the sweet, clean smell of the Swan River managed to penetrate our glass and metal confines.

'Let's play down the river,' I said suddenly. 'Dad's not going to bring us any chips. He won't notice we've gone.'

'We're supposed to stay in the car,' Jill said as she eyed me doubtfully.

'Look Jill, there's no use hoping he'll turn up with something. He's forgotten about us again. I'm going whether you come or not.'

The thought of a paddle was too much for Billy, who leapt out with me. Jill followed, reluctantly. We wound our way through the crowded car-park down to the sandy foreshore. We splashed and laughed and built sandcastles decorated with bits of seaweed.

Just as we were constructing an elaborate moat, a tall figure loomed above the beach. 'What the hell are you kids doing down here? I told you to stay in the car.' Dad advanced menacingly, and we froze.

Suddenly, I yelled, 'Well, what did ya expect us to do, sit in the car all night? You've been gone for ages *and* ya didn't give us any chips!' I stopped abruptly, my mouth wide open. Where had my sudden bravery come from? Now I'd done it.

Dad was as surprised as me. He stood looking down at us. His gaze took in three haphazard sandcastles and the beginning of an elaborate irrigation system. Without another word, he ushered us quietly to the car and took us home.

Dad's family often came to our place for Christmas lunch. Actually, I always found the two days before Christmas more exciting. Mum and Nan cooked cakes and puddings, gave the house a real good clean, and prepared the stuffing for the chickens. I was so excited. We only ate chicken once a year, and I loved it.

On the twenty-fourth of December, Dad would stride to the chook shed, armed with the axe. He always looked really determined, and I would sit and think that maybe this year he'd do it. About ten minutes would pass, then he'd stride back again, with a clean axe and no chooks. War had spoilt him for killing anything. He'd walk past me and hand the axe to Nan, who'd be patiently waiting on the back verandah: 'I can't do it Dais, you'll have to.'

Nan had a special relationship with the birds and chooks we kept, but she knew we were too poor to be able to consider her finer feelings. Within a few minutes, she'd be back with two limp chooks and a bloody axe. 'Come on Sal, time to gut.'

She'd spread newspaper over an old table we had on the back verandah and we'd set to work. I liked pulling out the feathers, because I was keen to collect those. Jill would walk past and eye us both in disgust. Sometimes, to scare her, I'd thrust a bloodied arm in her direction, and she'd scream and run inside to Mum.

'Aah, she's got no guts.'

'Well these chooks have, you get on with your work and leave poor Jilly alone!'

One Christmas, Grandpa told us all about the history of his family. 'Aah, yes,' he sighed as he downed another cold one, 'the Milroy men have always been great gamblers and drinkers. In the early days, we were quite well off. Had a business in Albany, coffee palace it was. You could make plenty of money then with all the migrants that were comin' into the country. As soon as the sailing ships docked, all the owners of boarding-houses, pubs, you name it, would rush down to the harbour to try and capture the trade. "Come to my place," one of them would call. "A free drink with every feed and a lolly for the little-uns," another might shout. "Double helpings of pud to all the men. Anything you want, we got!" Aah, the company was rough and ready, but business was booming. They all made a fortune, every last one. All except your great-grandfather, he never got past the pub halfway down the main street!'

I suppose it's not surprising that I developed a keen interest in drinking and smoking at a young age. I was adept at rolling Dad's cigarettes then passing them to him to light. I could pour a glass of beer with no head on it in a few seconds. Dad encouraged me to sip from his glass; Mum protested in vain. If she complained about the same thing too often, Dad would go out of his way to annoy her. He was a rebellious man.

Fortunately, it wasn't long before the taste of beer sickened me. I decided that was one tradition I wasn't going to maintain.

The day Uncle Frank entered our lives, I felt I'd found a kindred spirit. He just blew in out of nowhere one day. Dad was very pleased to see him.

Mum groaned as she eyed the brown paper bag tucked snugly under Frank's muscly arm. 'That's all Bill needs, more grog. You kids go out the back and play,' Mum commanded as Dad and Frank plonked themselves on the front porch. 'He's got the most dreadful language,' Mum whispered to Nan, 'I don't want the children hearing talk like that.'

My ears instantly pricked up. What dreadful language?

'Out you go, Sally,' Mum repeated.

'Okay, okay, I'm going,' I sighed as I nipped down the back verandah steps. It took only a few seconds for me to run around to the front of the house, where I happily joined the men on the porch.

Within a few minutes, Frank had me totally fascinated. He used so many words I'd never heard before, and they all sounded exciting. I'd have given anything to be able to talk like Frank.

'Young lady,' said Frank as he drained his glass, 'do ya know this father of yours saved my life during the war?'

'Give it a rest, Frank,' Dad groaned.

I leant forward eagerly, in the hope that Frank would continue. Suddenly, Mum popped her head around the front door. 'Sally, you come inside right now!' I gave her a grin and turned back to face Frank. 'Sally,' she whispered in a more determined way, 'come inside.'

Dad hated it when Mum began whispering from the doorway. He knew she kept her voice down because of the neighbours, so he said loudly, 'She's all right!' Dad didn't give a damn what the neighbours thought. Mum admitted defeat and disappeared back behind the door.

Frank grinned. 'Aah, yes, your father's a silly bastard, doesn't like me telling this story. We were both poor bastards stuck on a POW transport bound for the camps, Italian job she was, when *Boom!* a Pommy sub got us right up the Mediterranean! It was no picnic, I can tell you. Anyhow, we stayed afloat and beached on the Greek coast. I couldn't move, I was wounded in the chest. I thought I'd cashed in me chips. Then ya know what happened?'

'No, what?' I whispered.

'This bastard' — he jerked his thumb towards Dad — 'heaved me over his shoulder, dragged me up to the top deck and got me to shore. I was no lightweight then, either. I made bloody sure I got a look at his face before I passed out. I wasn't going to forget a bastard like that in a hurry.' Frank threw back his tight, curly head and roared laughing.

Like Frank, Dad was the kind of man who enjoyed defying the odds. I think it gave him a sense of power he didn't normally have. I'll never forget when, in September that year, he took us on a picnic to Roleystone. It was the only picnic I remember him taking us on. When he wasn't in hospital, he was rarely in a fit state to drive far, even if he wanted to.

All year, Mum had been promising us this picnic. We'd spent the May holidays playing down the swamp and visiting Dad in hospital. Now, halfway through the August holidays, we'd given up all hope of the picnic ever eventuating. So we were very surprised when, one sunny Saturday morning, Dad said, 'Right, we're off to the hills.'

We had an old 1948 Ford van by then. The Studebaker we had had for years was up on blocks in the drive; it was another one of those things Dad hadn't got around to fixing. The van had been a gift from one of Dad's old employers. When Dad was sober, he was a good worker, and it had been given to him in appreciation of a job well done.

The back of the van was completely open. The roof was padded with kapok; soft, fluffy pieces poked through the torn lining. In summer, the van was great, but in winter, the roof acted like a sponge, soaking up the rain and depositing lumps of soggy kapok into our laps. While we shouted our complaints from the back, Mum sat dry as a bone in the cab, giggling away. She'd confided to me that she'd learnt to laugh over difficult situations early in life, but I found this no comfort when it came to smelly, wet kapok.

The roads around Roleystone were narrow, steep and winding. Going for a picnic to the hills was no tame family outing: it was a real adventure.

Once we'd eaten our camp pie sandwiches and cake, we all ran screaming into the bush and spent hours collecting stones, insects, rocks and wildflowers. We knew that when we returned home, Nan would ask us what we'd found. She loved the bush, and always made us hand over any of our treasures that she thought could have special significance.

Too soon, Mum began shouting for us to return to the car. When we heard Dad tooting the horn, we knew he meant business. Billy, Jill and I leapt in the back, while Mum took her usual place in the front, holding our baby brother David on her lap.

It wasn't long before we realised what a difficult task Dad had trying to manoeuvre the van around on a tiny section of bitumen. He had a rough gravel track ahead of him, a cliff face on one side and a deep bush valley on the other. We all hung on tightly as he backed towards the edge of the bitumen, closer to the valley.

In sudden terror, we pressed as close to the cab as we could. With no back doors to hold us in, we feared that one sudden brake from Dad and we'd be catapulted into oblivion. To our horror, Dad failed to brake at all but continued to back closer and closer to the precipice. The wheels may have been on safe ground, but we felt practically airborne. Worse, the back of the van now sloped down, making it even more difficult for us to hold on. We began to scream.

'Shut up!' Dad roared as he poked his head out the side window. He edged a few inches more and we screamed louder.

'For God's sake, Bill, *stop!*' Mum shrieked. She was scared of heights. Her obvious panic incited us to greater efforts. We squashed our faces against the small window that separated the front cab from the back and, without taking a breath, we screamed as loud and as long as we could.

'Bill, *please*.'

'Listen, Glad, you stupid woman, I *know* what I'm doing!'

'Bill, *stop!* You can kill yourself if you want to, but you're not going to kill the rest of us!'

By this time, Dad had had enough. He pulled on the hand-brake and shouted, 'Get out, the bloody lot of you!'

We eagerly clambered to safety and stood in a nearby gully. We watched helplessly as Dad continued with what, we were sure, would be a death plunge. The back wheels rolled off the bitumen and spun on the loose gravel. There was a sudden roar of the engine as the van leapt forward and Dad neatly executed an awkward turn. With a look of smug satisfaction, he told us to get in.

Mum was quiet all the way home. Dad whistled.

4

PRETENDING

1959 and another Milroy began school. Billy's initial reaction was similar to mine; he hated it. Every morning when we set off for school, Billy lagged behind, sobbing. How he managed to walk straight always puzzled me, because while his body was trudging in the direction of school, his face was turned backwards towards our house. He knew Mum would be watching us from behind the curtains, and, if he looked really upset, she might weaken and call him back. Some days, he began his sobbing ritual so early that by the time we left, his face was red and puffy, his nose snotty and snorting. These occasions were generally too much for Mum, who only let him get as far as our letter-box before calling him back.

Billy's unhappiness at school never spilled over into recess and lunch-time. He was the kind of boy others looked up to, so he was never short of a pal. Billy was the image of Dad and, when it came to mateship, exactly like him.

Nan had a soft spot for Billy, too. 'Let him have the day off, Glad,' she pleaded when Billy began his crying routine, 'the child's not well.'

To Billy's credit, he didn't look well. I attempted to copy

his mournful look several times, but to no avail. After a few pathetic attempts, it became obvious that what worked for Billy would not work for me. I had to resort to more deceitful means.

I found that a light spattering of talcum powder, rubbed first into my hands and then patted lightly over my face, worked wonderfully well. 'I feel really sick in the stomach, Nan,' I groaned as she gazed at my pale face.

'Go and lie down,' Nan said. 'I'll send your mother in.'

Within a few minutes, Mum was standing by my bedside, looking extremely sceptical. 'Sally... are you *really* sick?'

Nan always interrupted. 'Course she's sick, Glad, look at the child's face.'

'I'm not puttin' it on, Mum, honest. I feel real crook.'

'All right,' Mum relented, 'you can stay home, but don't eat anything and stay in bed.'

Jill wandered in after Mum and Nan had left. 'You're rotten. You're not really sick, are you?'

'Course I am! Go away, you're makin' me feel sick. *Mu-um*, tell Jill to go away, she's makin' me feel worse.'

Once Jill and Billy had left for school, and Mum had left for her part-time job in Boans' Floral Department, I called out to Nan, 'I'm feelin' a bit better. Do ya think I could eat something?'

Nan pottered in with her old tea-towel slung over her shoulder. 'Oooh, you still look white, Sally. I don't think you eat enough, your mother can't expect you to get better if you're not going to eat. You stay there and I'll bring in some toast and a hot cup of tea.'

After six or so rounds of toast and jam and a couple of mugs of tea, I said to Nan, 'Gee, it's stuffy in here.'

'Go and sit outside, there's nothin' like a bit of fresh air when you're sick in the stomach.'

Nan only spoke to me after that to tell me when lunch was ready. I spent the rest of the day outdoors, playing games and climbing trees.

I was sitting on the back verandah step, inspecting the cache of small rocks I'd collected, when Mum returned home from her day at work.

'How's Sally?'

'Hmmph, she's all right,' Nan grumbled. And then, with a giggle, she added, 'Been sittin' in that tree all day.'

Mum wandered out. 'Another miraculous recovery, eh Sal?'

'Yeah, dunno what it was, Mum, but I hope I don't get it again.'

'Don't hope too much.'

The best thing about school was that Grades Two and Three shared the same room, so this meant I saw more of Jill.

One afternoon, our teacher asked if there were any children in the class who could sing in a foreign language. Four children immediately raised their hands, Jill and I included. At the teacher's instruction, the first two kids got up and sang *Frère Jacques*. Then it was Jill's and my turn. We were both very shy and embarrassed and walked to the front with our eyes down.

We linked arms and then, swaying energetically back and forth, loudly sang *The Internationale* in Italian. Dad had taught it to Jill as well.

Mrs White was as stunned as the rest of our class at our sudden show of theatrical talent. We usually shunned any form of public display. 'Lovely, girls,' she finally said, 'lovely.'

Dad was in hospital at the time so we were unable to tell him how we'd performed, but we knew that he would have been proud of us.

Whenever Dad was in hospital, Mum and Nan went out of their way to make home a nice place for us. We were allowed to stay up late, and we didn't have to worry about keeping quiet. It was much more relaxed.

Sometimes, Mum scraped together enough money to shout Jill, Billy and me to the local outdoor theatre. The theatre fascinated us. We loved the gaily striped canvas seats, the large spotlights and the huge white screen. It was such a magical place, we even felt excited during intermission.

But one of the best nights we had there was the time Mum provided the entertainment. After we paid our threepence entry fee, we walked up and down, searching for four empty seats. Mum reckoned we'd be lucky to find any, because they always sold more tickets than they had seats. Then Billy's keen eyes spotted four beauties.

'Over there, Mum,' he shouted.

Mum looked in the direction he was pointing and sighed: they were in the middle row of the centre block, almost impossible to get at. The rows were so narrow it was difficult to walk between them even when they were vacant. Only someone very brave would consider trying to claim them when all the surrounding seats were full, and, when one of our party happened to be a woman who was eight months pregnant...

'There must be somewhere else,' Mum said helplessly.

'There's not, Mum,' I said matter-of-factly. 'If we want to sit together, it'll have to be those.'

As we struggled over the various arms and legs jutting in our path, Mum kept apologising, 'I'm sorry, please excuse me...' By the time we reached the empty seats, she was blushing and exhausted.

It was halfway through a news item on the Queen Mother that Mum disappeared. There was a sudden rip, followed by an urgent gurgling noise. All we could see was her desperately flailing arms and legs. We managed to grasp her hands and tried the old heave-ho, to no avail. A sympathetic chap in front gave us a hand. As he pulled, we pushed. The newsreel rolled on to the Queen Mum's final wave. A lady kindly went to fetch the manager, and returned with the bouncer as well. When they reached Mum, she was a quivering, giggling mass and we were near hysteria.

By the end of the newsreel, Mum was free. Embarrassed, but free. She was supplied with a hard metal chair to sit on, and a small bottle of lime cool drink by way of compensation. She consoled herself that at least it hadn't been necessary to turn on the lights.

It was early in Grade Three that I developed my infallible Look At The Lunch method for telling which part of Manning my class-mates came from. I knew I came from the rough-and-tumble part, where there were teenage gangs called Bodgies and Widgies, and where hardly anyone looked after their garden.

There was another part of Manning that, before I'd started school, I had been unaware of. The residents preferred to call it Como. The houses were similar, only in better condition. The gardens were neat and tidy, and I'd heard there was carpet on the floors. Children from Como always had totally different lunches to children from Manning. Pieces of salad, chopped up and sealed in plastic containers. Their cake was wrapped neatly in greaseproof paper, and they had real cordial in a proper flask. There was a kid in our class whose parents were so wealthy he had bacon sandwiches for lunch.

By contrast, kids from Manning drank from the water fountain and carried sticky jam sandwiches in brown paper bags.

Nan normally made our sandwiches for school. She made them very neatly; sometimes she even cut the crusts off. I was convinced that made our sandwiches special. There were occasions when Mum took over the sandwich-making. Her lunches stand out in my mind as beacons of social embarrassment. With a few deft strokes, she could carve the most unusual slabs of bread. These would then be glued together with thick chunks of hardened butter and globules of jam or Vegemite. Both, if she forgot to clean the knife between sandwiches. We always felt relieved when, once again, Nan assumed the sandwich-making role.

In April that year, my youngest sister, Helen, was born. I found myself taking an interest in her because at least she had the good sense not to be born on my birthday. There were five of us now; I wondered how many more kids Mum was going to squeeze into the house. Someone at school had told me that babies were found under cabbage leaves. I was glad we never grew cabbages.

Each year, our house seemed to get smaller. In my room, we had two single beds lashed together and a double kapok mattress plonked on top. Jill, Billy and I slept in there, sometimes David too, and, more often than not, Nan as well. I loved that mattress. Whenever I lay on it, I imagined I was sinking into a bed of feathers, just like a fairy princess.

The kids at school were amazed to hear that I shared a bed with my brother and sister. I never told them about the times we'd squeezed five in that bed. All my class-mates had their own beds; some even had their own rooms. I considered them disadvantaged. I couldn't explain the happy feeling of warm security I felt when we all snuggled in together.

Also, I found some of their attitudes to their brothers and sisters hard to understand. They didn't seem to really like one another, and you never caught them together at school. We were just the opposite. Billy, Jill and I always spoke in the playground and we often walked home together, too. We felt our family was the most important thing in the world. One of the girls in my class said accusingly one day: 'Aah, you lot stick like glue.' *You're right*, I thought, *we do*.

The kids at school had also begun asking us what country we came from. This puzzled me because, up until then, I'd thought we were the same as them. If we insisted that we came from Australia, they'd reply, 'Yeah, but what about ya parents, bet they didn't come from Australia.'

One day, I tackled Mum about it as she washed the dishes.

'What do you mean, "Where do we come from?"'

'The kids at school want to know what country we come from. They reckon we're not Aussies.'

Mum was silent. Nan grunted in a cross sort of way, then got up from the table and walked outside.

'Come on, Mum, what are we?'

'What do the kids at school say?'

'Italian, Greek, Indian...'

'Tell them you're Indian.'

'Are we really? Indian!' It sounded so exotic. 'When did we come here?'

'A long time ago,' Mum replied. 'Now, no more questions. You just tell them you're Indian.'

It was good to have an answer and it satisfied our playmates. They could quite believe we were Indian; they just didn't want us pretending we were Aussies when we weren't.

5

ONLY A DREAM

By the time I was eight-and-a-half, an ambulance parked at the front of our house was a neighbourhood tradition. It would come belting down our street, siren blaring, and halt abruptly at our front gate. The ambulance officers knew just how to manage Dad. Usually, Dad teetered out awkwardly by himself, with the officers on either side offering token support. Other times, as when his left lung collapsed, he went out on a grey-blanketed stretcher.

Jill, Billy and I accepted his comings and goings with the innocent selfishness of children. We never doubted he'd be back.

Dad hated being in hospital. I heard him telling Mum about how he'd woken up in hospital one night, screaming. He thought he'd been captured again. There was dirt in his mouth and a rifle butt in his back. He tried to get up, but he couldn't move. Next thing he knew, the night sister was flicking a torch in his eyes. 'All tangled up again are we, Mr Milroy? It's only a dream, you know. No need to upset yourself.'

Dad laughed when he told Mum what the sister had said. Only a dream, I thought. I was just a kid, and I knew it wasn't a dream.

When Dad got really bad, our only way out was a midnight flit to Aunty Grace's house. Other nights, the five of us were shut up in one room; sometimes, Mum put Helen and David, the babies of the family, to bed in the back of the van. I was so envious. I complained strongly to Mum, 'It's not fair! Why can't I sleep in the van?' I never realised that if we had to leave the house suddenly, the babies would be the most difficult to wake up.

Aunty Grace, a civilian widow, lived at the back of us. Nan had knocked out six pickets in the back fence so we could easily run from our yard to hers. Many times, we were quietly woken in the dark and bundled off to Grace's house.

'Sally...wake up. Get out of bed, but be very quiet.'

'Aw, not again, Nan.' It had been a bad two weeks.

'Your mother's waiting in the yard, you go out there while I wake Billy and Jill.'

I walked quickly through the kitchen, scuttled across the verandah and into the shadows, where Mum was standing with the babies. She was rocking Helen to stop her from crying and David was leaning against her legs, half-asleep. Nan shuffled down the steps with Billy and Jill, and we were on our way.

'No talking, you kids,' Mum said, 'stay close.'

We followed the line of shadows to the rear of our yard. Just as we neared the gap in the back picket fence, Dad flung open the door of his sleepout and staggered onto the verandah, yelling abuse.

Oh no, I thought, he's gunna come and get us! We all crouched down and hid behind some bushes. I prayed Helen wouldn't cry. I hardly breathed. I was sure Dad would hear me if I did. I would feel terrible if my breathing led him to where we were all hiding. I remembered the stories Dad had told me about the camps he'd been in. Horse's Head Soup. They'd had Horse's Head Soup and the men fought over the eye because it was the only bit of meat. I was shivering, I didn't know whether it was from nerves or cold. I remembered then that the Germans had stripped Dad naked and forced him to stand for hours in the snow. My heart was pounding. I suddenly understood what it had been like for Dad and his friends; they'd felt just the way I was feeling now. Alone, and very frightened.

For some reason, Dad stopped yelling and swearing; he turned and shuffled back to his room.

'Now, kids,' Mum said. We didn't need to be told twice. With unusual speed, Billy, Jill and I darted through the gap to safety.

Within seconds, we were all grouped around Grace's wood stove, cooking toast and waiting for our cup of tea. I felt safe now. Had I really been so terrified only a moment ago? It was a different world.

We never stayed at Aunty Grace's long, just until Dad was back on an even keel. Prior to our return, I would be sent to negotiate with him. 'He'll listen to you,' they said. Nan walked me to the gap in the picket fence. After that I was on my own. One night, I told Nan I didn't want to go. 'You must, there's no one else,' she replied. She stood in the gap and watched me until I reached the back verandah.

My father's room was the sleepout; his light burnt all hours. I think he disliked the dark as much as me.

I wondered if I'd find something horrible when I got there. I didn't, there was only Dad sitting on his hard, narrow bed, surrounded by empties. He always knew when I had come, and quietly opened his bedroom door when he heard the creak on the back verandah.

I took up my usual position on the end of his bed. The grey blanket I sat on was rough, and I plucked at it nervously.

Dad sat with shoulders hunched. His hair curled forward, one persistent lock drooping over his brow and partly obscuring three deep parallel wrinkles. They reminded me of marks left in damp dirt after Nan had dug her spade in. It was on the tip of my tongue to ask, who dug your wrinkles, Dad? I knew it would make him cry. When Dad smiled, his eyes crinkled at the corners. It was nice. He wasn't smiling now, just waiting.

'Dad, we'll all come back if you'll be good,' I stated matter-of-factly. I'd inherited none of Mum's natural diplomacy, but I sensed that Dad hated being alone, so I started from there. He responded with his usual brief, wry smile, then gave me his usual answer: 'I'll let you all come back as long as your grandmother doesn't.' He had a thing about Nanna.

'You know we won't come back without her, Dad,' I said firmly. How would Mum cope with him on her own? And anyway, where would Nan go?

Dad ran his hand through his hair. It was a characteristic gesture; he was thinking. Reaching behind his back and down the side of his bed, he pulled out three unopened packets of potato chips. Slowly, he placed them one by one in my lap. I could feel the pointed corner of one pack sticking through the cotton of my thin summer dress into my thigh. Suddenly my mouth was full of water.

'You can have them all,' he said quietly, 'if...you stay with me.'

Dad looked at me and I looked at the chips. They were a rare treat. Reluctantly I handed them back. I was surprised Dad was trying to bribe me, I knew that he knew it was wrong.

'I always thought you liked your mother better than me.' He didn't really mean it, it was just another ploy to get me to stay. Deep down, he understood my decision. Reaching up, he opened the door and I walked out onto the verandah. *Click* went the lock and I was alone.

Maybe if I waited for a while, he would call me back. I squatted on the bare verandah.

Some sixth sense must have told Dad I was still there; his bedroom door suddenly opened and light streamed out, illuminating my small hunched figure. Towering over me, Dad yelled, 'What the hell do you think you're doing here? GET GOING!'

I shot down the three back steps, leapt through the gap in the back picket fence and arrived panting at the door of Aunty Grace's laundry.

Mum and Nan always questioned me in detail about what Dad said. It was never any different, he always said the same thing. Once I'd finished telling them, they'd then ask me how he seemed. I found that a difficult question to answer, because Dad was more aggressive towards them than he was towards me.

The following day, we generally returned home. I guess Dad slept it off.

There was only one occasion when Dad intruded into our sanctuary. We were sitting in Grace's kitchen when he appeared unexpectedly in the doorway. We were all stunned. No one was sure what was going to happen. For some reason, Dad didn't seem to know what to do, either. He looked at all of us in a desperate kind of way, then fixed his gaze on Mum. I heard him mumble something indistinct, but Mum didn't reply. She just stood there, holding the teapot, frozen. I think it was her lack of response that forced him to turn to me.

'All right, Sally, which one of us do you love the most? Choose which one of us you want to live with, your mother or me.'

I was as shocked as Mum. I wanted to shout, 'Don't do this to me, I'm only a kid!' but nothing came out.

Dad stayed a few seconds longer, then, in a resigned tone, he muttered, 'I knew you'd choose her,' and left as quickly as he'd come.

He was so lost. I blamed myself for being too young.

6

A CHANGE

Halfway through second term of my fourth year at school I suddenly discovered a friend. Our teacher began reading stories about Winnie the Pooh every Wednesday. From then on, I was never sick on Wednesdays. In a way, discovering Pooh was my salvation. He made me feel more normal. I suppose I saw something of myself in him.

Pooh lived in a world of his own and he believed in magic, the same as me. He wasn't particularly good at anything, but everyone loved him, anyway. I was fascinated by the way he could make an adventure out of anything, even tracks in the snow. And while Pooh was obsessed with honey, I was obsessed with drawing.

When I couldn't find any paper or pencils, I would fish small pieces of charcoal from the fire and tear strips off the paperbark tree in our yard, and draw on that. I drew in the sand, on the footpath, the road, even on the walls when Mum wasn't looking. One day, a neighbour gave me a batch of oil paints left over from a stint in prison. I felt like a real artist.

My drawings were very personal. I hated anyone watching me draw. I didn't even like people seeing my drawings when they were finished. I drew for myself, not anyone else. One day, Mum asked me why I always drew sad things. I hadn't realised until then that my drawings were sad. I was shocked to see my feelings glaring up at me from the page. I became even more secretive after that.

Dad never took any interest in my drawings, he was completely enveloped in his own world. He never went to the pub now; we couldn't afford the petrol. There was no money for toys, clothes, furniture, barely enough for food, but always plenty for Dad's beer. Everything valuable had been hocked.

One day, Dad was so desperate he raided our little tin money-boxes and removed all our hard-won threepenny bits. What was even more upsetting was that he'd opened them at the bottom, then placed them back on the shelf as though they'd never been tampered with. Jill and I kept putting our money in and he kept taking it out. 'Who knows how long we've been supplying him!' I complained to Mum. I felt really hurt; if Dad had asked me, I'd have given him the contents, willingly.

As usual, Mum saw the funny side of things.

'How can you think it's funny?' I demanded.

'Can't you see the funny side? It was such a childish thing to do.'

I didn't think it was funny. He was just like a child, sometimes, he never mended anything around the house, or took any responsibility. I felt very disappointed in him.

Dad hated being poor, and I could forgive him for that, because I hated it myself. He loved the luxuries working-class people couldn't afford. If he had been able to, he would have given us anything. Instead, his craving for beer and his illness left us with nothing. I knew that Mum and Dad had had dreams once. It wasn't supposed to have turned out like this.

That year, Dad's love of luxuries really broke our budget, but it also gave us the status of being the first family in our street to have television.

As he carried it in, an awkward-looking square on four pointy legs, and tried to manoeuvre it through the front door, we all rushed at him excitedly. 'Get out the way, you kids,' he yelled as he staggered into the hall. Televisions were heavy in those days. The hallowed object was finally set down in the lounge-room.

We lined up in awe behind Dad, waiting for our first glimpse of this modern-day miracle. We were disappointed. All we saw was white flecks darting across a grey screen, all we heard was a buzzing noise. Dad realised the rental people had forgotten to leave the aerial.

The aerial arrived the following day. Grey, human-like figures became discernible and their conversations with one another audible, but they didn't impress me. I had the feeling they weren't quite sure of whatever it was they were supposed to be doing.

In July, we had a surprise visit. We were all playing happily outside when Mum called us in. When we reached the hall, I stopped dead in my tracks. Mum grinned at me and said, 'Say hello, these are your cousins.' As usual, my mouth had difficulty working. The small group of dark children stared at me. They seemed shy, too.

Then a very tall, dark man walked in and patted me on the head. He had the biggest smile I'd ever seen. 'This is Arthur,' Mum said proudly, 'Nanna's brother.' I stared at him in shock. I didn't know she had a brother.

Arthur returned to the lounge-room and we kids all sat on the floor, giggling behind our hands and staring at one another. Mum slipped into the kitchen to make a cup of tea. I glimpsed her going into Dad's room.

Mum said, very brightly, to Arthur, 'He's asleep. Perhaps he'll wake up before you leave.' I knew she was lying, but I didn't understand why.

After a while, they all left. I was surprised Arthur spoke English. I thought maybe he could speak English and Indian, whereas the kids probably only spoke Indian.

I don't remember ever seeing them again while I was a child, but the image of their smiling faces lodged deep in my memory. I often wondered about them. I wanted them to teach me Indian. I never said anything to Mum. I knew, instinctively, that if I asked about them, she wouldn't tell me anything.

Dad seemed to be getting sicker and sicker. By the time September came around, he had been in hospital more than he'd been home.

One morning he emerged from his room early. We were just finishing breakfast. All the previous week he'd been in hospital, so we were surprised by the cheery look on his face. Nan hovered near the table, intent on hurrying us along.

'Come on, you kids, you'll be late,' she grumbled.

'Aw, let them stay home, Dais,' Dad said. 'I'll look after them.' Had I heard right? I froze halfway through my last slice of toast and jam. I'd heard him call Nan 'Dais' before. It was his way of charming her. Her name was Daisy.

Nan was as surprised as me. She flicked her dirty tea-towel towards us and muttered in her grumpiest voice, 'They have to go to school, Bill, they can't stay home.' I sensed that she was unsure of herself; she eyed Dad shrewdly.

'Well, let little Billy stay then, Dais,' Dad coaxed. I smiled. He'd called her Dais again; how could she resist?

Nan relented. 'All right. Just Billy. Now, off you girls go!'

Billy waved at us smugly. Jill and I grumbled. Nan had always favoured the boys in our family, and now Dad was doing the same.

By lunch-time, we'd forgotten all about Billy. Jill and I were helping to paint curtains for Parents' Night, held at the end of each year. We were halfway through drawing a black swan family when the Headmaster came down and told us we could go home early. We were puzzled, but very pleased to be leaving before the other kids.

Nan wasn't happy when she saw us shuffling up the footpath.

'What are you kids doing here? They were supposed to keep you late at school. Go outside and play.'

Jill immediately raced out the back to play with Billy, but I decided I'd like something to eat first. I was just coming out of the kitchen with a Vegemite sandwich when the familiar sound of an ambulance siren drew me to the front door. Nan stood impatiently on the porch, her hand over her mouth. When she saw me, she turned crossly and said, 'I told you to go out the back!'

Two ambulance men hurried up the path. A stretcher case, I noted, as they walked briskly through. In a few minutes, they returned. I watched as they carried Dad carefully but quickly down our faded red footpath. This time, I couldn't see his face.

Billy, Jill and David pushed up behind me, followed by Mrs Mainwaring, our neighbour. Before I knew it, she'd ushered us into the lounge-room and told us to sit down, as she had something important to say. It was then that I noticed Mum squashed in the old cane chair in the corner of the room. Nan hovered beside her, stuffing handkerchiefs into her hand.

'What are ya crying for, Mum?' I asked, puzzled. She'd never cried when Dad had gone before. I tried to reassure her by saying confidently, 'He always comes back,' at which, she broke down completely and hid her face in a striped grey handkerchief.

'Please sit down, Sally,' said Mrs Mainwaring. 'I have something to tell you all.' I obeyed instantly. She was a nice middle-aged lady and we were a little in awe of her. Her home was very neat. 'Now,' she continued. 'I have some bad news for you all.' She paused and took a deep breath.

'He's dead, isn't he?' I was sure I said it out loud, but I couldn't have, because everyone ignored me.

'He's dead, isn't he?' I repeated. Still no response. My heart was pounding. Mrs Mainwaring's lips were moving, but I couldn't hear a word. He was dead. I knew it. Dad was gone.

'...Now children, I want you all to go to your rooms.' Somehow, this sentence managed to penetrate my numbed brain. I looked around at my brothers and sisters. No one was moving. I craned my neck to look at Mum. She was avoiding my gaze. We all looked blank. What were we going to do in our rooms?

Mrs Mainwaring finally pulled each one of us up and ushered us out. As I closed the bedroom door, Jill said, 'What are we s'posed to do?'

I was shocked; it wasn't like her not to know what the right thing was. With the superior confidence of a nine-year-old, I flung myself stomach-down on the bed and said, 'I s'pose we'd better cry.'

We cried for what seemed a long time, then our bedroom door slowly opened and Billy's freckled face peered around. 'I'm going outside, who wants to come and play?'

'You horrible boy,' I growled, 'don't you know he's dead?' After all, he'd been with Dad all day. Billy vanished.

'He doesn't understand.' Jill defended him as usual. 'He doesn't know what he's s'posed to do.'

We lay on our beds a few moments longer. I began to count the fly specks on the ceiling.

'Sally...do ya think...we could...go outside and play now?' Jill asked.

'You're as bad as Billy.'

'Well, at least I cried. That wasn't easy, you know.' Jill put her head under her arm. I watched her silently.

'Oh, come on then,' I said. And leaping up, we joined Billy in the yard.

7

FAMILY AND FRIENDS

I felt very strongly about families sticking together. So strongly, in fact, that I had a secret meeting with my brothers and sisters; for some reason, I was frightened we would be put in an orphanage. I'd read about such things and I was determined it wouldn't happen to us. We pledged to run away together if it looked like happening.

We needn't have worried. A couple of weeks after Dad died, Mum informed us that Billy was now the man of the house. This came as a great surprise. Billy was only six years old.

Billy took Mum's Man Of The House thing very seriously. For example, whenever anything broke down, he insisted it was his job to fix it. But whenever Billy fixed anything, Mum ended up having to pay out money. So much so that when he accidentally locked himself in the toilet, she felt like leaving him there.

'I'm sure he'll grow up to be a great inventor,' Mum said after she let him out. 'He's so interested in the way things go together.' I just grinned and listed the clock, the toaster, Dad's old watch and David's clockwork train, all now in pieces. Mum laughed. 'Well, he has to practise on something.'

Whenever one of us mentioned Dad's death, Mum would say, 'Never mind, Billy's the Man Of The House now. He'll look after us, won't you, Billy?' It was an old-fashioned thought: Billy, the eldest son. I think Mum meant to reassure us with her statements, but she only confused us. We wondered if Billy had special powers we didn't know about.

A few months after Dad's death, Mum found out the contents of the Coroner's Report. The verdict was suicide. Mum was very upset. She had told us all that the war had killed Dad. She'd fixed it into our minds that Dad's death was due to something called War Causes.

The coroner attributed Dad's suicide to the after-effects of war, and that meant there were no problems with Mum obtaining a war pension, regular money at a time when we needed it.

Fear had suddenly vanished from our lives. There were no more midnight flits to Aunty Grace's house, no more hospitals, no more ambulances. We were on our own, but peace had returned. I was still afraid of the dark, but I didn't burrow under my pillow any more.

Dad's death crystallised many things for me. I decided that, when I grew up, I would never drink or marry a man who drank. The smell of alcohol, especially beer, made me feel sick. I also decided that I would never be poor. It wasn't that I was ashamed of the way we lived, it was just that I longed for things I knew only money could buy. Art paper and paints, piano lessons, a pink nylon dress, bacon sandwiches...

We saw very little of Dad's brothers during those early months. One uncle gave Mum what he thought was good advice. 'Glad,' he said, 'a good-looking woman like you, in your position, there's only one thing ya can do. Find a bloke and live with him. If you're lucky, he might take the kids as well.' Another uncle turned up a few weeks later and drove off in our only asset, the 1948 Ford van. He reasoned that as Mum didn't have her driver's licence she wouldn't be needing it.

Mum was pretty down after that. 'Men,' she told us cynically, 'they're useless, no good for anything!'

If it hadn't been for Uncle Frank, we probably would have gone along with Mum's theory. Mind you, she wasn't too pleased at first when he showed up.

'G'day, Glad,' he said when she answered the front door, 'just brought this around for ya. How ya goin', kids?' He grinned as we appeared behind Mum in the doorway. 'We'll have to go out one day. Well, better get goin'. 'Bye, Glad.' Mum smiled and closed the door.

'What you got there?' Nan said as she poked in the box. 'Chicken, eh? And vegetables.'

I couldn't believe it was real chicken, such a luxury. I don't think Mum could believe it, either. Frank, of all people — she'd thought he was just another boozer.

To our surprise, Frank came around the following weeks with the same thing. Then Mum found out that the Raffles Hotel was holding a weekly lottery. The prize was always a box of fruit and vegetables and a fresh chicken, and the winner was always Uncle Frank.

Frank gave us more than just a helping hand. He introduced his wife to Mum and they became good friends. Aunty Lorna had a little car and she took us for picnics in the bush. She always packed a delicious lunch.

Frank encouraged Mum to have driving lessons. He was a bit of a mechanic in his spare time. He said he'd fix the van — for some reason, my uncle had returned it. Mum said she'd heard that other blokes had made comments to him.

Pretty soon, Mum got her licence, then she and Lorna took it in turns to drive to the hills. Mum also began to make regular visits to Grandma and Grandpa's house. I think she was hoping they'd take an interest in us kids, but it didn't really work out like that. The only one they were really keen on was Billy, and that was only because he was the image of Dad. Grandpa always liked to have Billy close to him, but the rest of us were relegated to the backyard. Our cousins were allowed inside, but we had to stay outside.

Being outdoors at their place wasn't much fun. There was no bush near Grandma and Grandpa's, and no old bikes or toys. Finally, Mum would come out with a tray of drinks and a piece of cake for each of us. After that, we knew it was time to go home.

It wasn't that our grandparents disliked us. After all, half of us belonged to Dad. It was the other half they were worried about.

It took only a few months for our regular visits to cease. Sometimes, we bumped into Grandpa in town. He would cry when he saw Billy. I remember once he actually tried to apologise to Mum for Grandma's attitude. 'What can I do, Glad. Ya know what she's like.' Mum just shrugged her shoulders.

Somehow Mum managed to hang on to the television after Dad died. There were other things we needed in our house far more desperately, but the TV did more for us than warm clothes or extra beds ever could. It gave us a way out. We got into the habit of making up rough beds on the floor of the lounge-room. Mum stoked up the fire, and, snuggled beneath our coats and rugs, we became enraptured in movies of the twenties, thirties and forties. Apart from romantic musicals, we were very fond of war movies. Mum often said, 'Your father fought there,' or, 'I remember your father telling me about that place.' Sometimes, one of the actors would look like Dad, and I'd try and pretend it was him, living out an earlier part of his life on the screen. But the glamorous heroism portrayed in the movies seemed far removed from what I'd heard Dad describe.

When television finished for the evening, Mum made us all hot cups of sweet tea and toast with jam or Vegemite. We stoked up the fire and swapped yarns and stories until the early hours of the morning. Sometimes, we had a singalong — those went on for hours. We only stopped when we fell asleep or were too hoarse to sing any more.

I'll never forget those evenings, the open fire, Mum and Nan, all of us laughing and joking. I felt very secure. I knew it was us against the world, but I also knew that, as long as

I had my family, I'd make it.

I had little idea how hard that first year was for Mum and Nan. Mum was thirty-one when Dad died, and she had five of us to rear. I was nine years old; Helen, the youngest, was only eighteen months.

Mum didn't like leaving us, but she knew that if we were ever to get ahead, she would have to work. Mum was never afraid to work. She had always kept some money coming in all the years Dad was sick; now she increased her load and took on whatever jobs were going. It was difficult to find full-time employment, so she accepted numerous part-time positions.

I remember, at one stage, we were really desperate. Mum and Nan kept talking in whispers. They decided to write a letter to Alice Drake-Brockman in Sydney to see if her family could lend us some money. They were really disappointed when the reply came; it said that they were broke, too, and couldn't lend us anything. Nan was very bitter. She said she didn't care that they were bankrupt, they owed her. I didn't know what she was talking about.

Besides good old Uncle Frank, the other saviour of our family at this time was Legacy. All fatherless families of returned soldiers were assigned a Legatee, a gentleman of good community standing who had a soft spot for children. Ours proved to be a kindly older man with only one child of his own. His name was Mr Wilson; we affectionately shortened it to Mr Willie.

Mr Willie got into the habit of taking us to the beach, and on picnics and barbecues. He had what we considered a really flash car, and we always felt very special when we rode in it. He told us he would be taking us to all the Legacy outings, and he also informed us that we would all have to take part in the Anzac Day march once a year.

'Why do we have to march?' I asked him one day.

'Because your father was a soldier. All children who belong to soldiers have to march. People need to be reminded of the legacy the war has left. And anyway, your father was a brave man, you should march to honour him.'

I wasn't keen to remind people of the war, but I couldn't fault his argument about Dad.

8

WILDLIFE

In no time at all, our house became inundated with pets. Cats, dogs, budgies, rabbits and, of course, the chickens — any stray creature found a home with us. When our cat population hit thirteen, Mum decided it was too much and found homes for half of them. Then my white rabbit escaped, one of the dogs was run over, and another cat went wild.

The dog we lost had been an old and treasured member of the family. I decided we needed another dog to replace him, so I persuaded Mum to look around some local pet shops.

'We won't buy one, Mum, we'll just look.'

'No more animals, Sally.'

'I know, Mum. But can't we look?'

'All right. It'll be an outing for you kids.'

A pet shop nearby had six adorable kelpie-cross pups. We all huddled around their cage in awe as they licked our fingers and looked at us appealingly.

'That one,' I said to Mum, as I eyed the largest pup. 'We'll take that one, Mum.'

'I'm not buying a dog, Sally. I've hardly got enough money to feed what we've got without adding to it.'

'That one's older than the others,' interrupted the

shopkeeper.

'No one seems to want him.' It was the best thing he could have said.

'You see, Mum, no one wants him. What'll become of him?'

'I'm not buying him.'

'Can I take him out of the cage and hold him, Mum? It might be the only cuddle he ever gets.'

'Good idea, little lady,' said the storekeeper enthusiastically as he opened the cage.

I lifted the pup out. He was gangly and awkward. 'Isn't he beautiful?' I held him up to Mum.

'Just look at the size of his paws! They're huge! No, Sally, he'll be a big boy when he's fully grown.'

'But Mum, we've never had a big dog.'

'Please, Mum,' pleaded my brothers and sisters.

'We-ll.' Mum sighed as the pup gave her a lick.

'Be a good guard dog, Mum,' said Billy.

'I'll let you have him for half-price,' coaxed the storekeeper.

Mum groaned. 'Oh, all right, we'll take him.'

We named the pup Blackie, because he was mostly black. A few weeks later, we renamed him Widdles.

One night, Mum complained about this new name. 'I feel silly calling out "Widdles" when I want him to come for his tea. The neighbours are all laughing.' From then on, whenever Mum wanted him, she shouted out, 'Here, Widdees, here, boy.' The neighbours still laughed, but in Mum's mind it made some sort of difference.

The only pets we weren't allowed to keep were wild ones. Goannas, tadpoles, frogs, gilgies* and insects all had to be returned alive and well to their natural habitat. Nan influenced us greatly when it came to our attitudes to the wildlife around us.

* *gilgie* — a small fresh-water crayfish. (Known in other parts of Australia as a yabby.)

Our lives revolved around her, now. She kept the home fires burning while Mum worked three part-time jobs. Nan did the cooking, cleaning, washing, ironing and mending, as well as chopping all our wood and looking after the garden. The kitchen had become her domain and she disliked us kids intruding. 'You kids get out of my kitchen,' she'd yell as she flicked a tea-towel towards us. We offered to help, but she sent us outside to play.

Nan fostered our interest in the local wildlife by showing great concern for any new creature we brought home from the swamp. Frogs and goannas seemed to be her favourites. One afternoon, I discovered a big, fat bobtail goanna curled up under a bit of rusty tin against the wall of our chook shed.

'Jill, come quick, look what I've found.' We both lay stomach-down in the dirt and stared into its glassy eyes for ages.

When Nan found us, she said, 'What are you kids up to?'

'It's a goanna, Nan. Look.'

'Oooh, he's fat,' Nan exclaimed. 'Now you kids leave him there. He can live there if he wants. Don't you go hurtin' him.'

'Course we're not gunna hurt him,' I said indignantly. 'Can we feed him, Nan?'

'No need to, he'll find his own tucker.'

I thought that was a bit mean. I decided I'd like to tame that goanna, so that night after tea, I crept out with a bit of stale cake. I slid it under the tin, and then, in a quiet voice, I let the goanna know who had put it there. After all, I didn't want him palling up with someone who hadn't even gone to the trouble of feeding him.

The next morning, my friend had disappeared. Nan came over to check on him and found me squatting in the sand with a puzzled expression on my face.

'That goanna still there?'

'Naah, he's gone. I wanted him for a pet.'

'I bet he's hiding farther back. He doesn't want us to see him. Look out, I'll move the tin along a bit.' I slid back in the dirt and Nan slowly moved the tin. No goanna.

'How did this get here?' Nan asked. In her hand was the stale bit of yellow cake I'd put there the night before.

'Thought he might be hungry,' I replied guiltily.

'Told you he could get his own tucker. You've scared him off now.'

Nan explained to me that it wasn't the right kind of food for a goanna.

I just nodded. I was convinced he'd had a nibble of Mum's cake and crawled away to die. I felt awful. It was a terrible thing to have the poisoning of a goanna on your conscience.

Walking home late one afternoon, I heard an urgent call coming from the bush nearby. I stopped dead in my tracks. There it was again, a frantic *Cheep! Cheep!* I walked carefully into the bush until I came to a small clearing; there, at the base of a tall white gum tree, was a tiny baby mudlark. I stepped back and looked up at the branches high above. Amongst the leaves, I could glimpse the dark outline of a small nest. I knew there was no chance of returning him up there, it was far too high, and, even if I did, the mother might smell human on her baby and kick him out. There was only one thing I could do — take him home.

When Mum saw the bulge in the pocket of my dress, she sighed. 'Oh no, what have you got there?'

I showed her the bird. 'I'm going to call him Muddy,' I said optimistically. I knew Mum was fed up with me bringing home strays.

'I told you, Sally, no more pets. I'm the one that ends up feeding them.'

'But he's only a baby. I promise I'll look after him.'

'What have you got there?' Nan said as she entered the fray.

'It's a baby mudlark, Nan, fell out of a tree. Mum wants to kick it out.'

'Sally, I do not!'

'Then you'll let me keep it?'

'Oh...all right, but I'm not having anything to do with it. There might be something wrong with it. I've heard of mother birds getting rid of babies for that reason. He might not live, he's very small.'

'Hmmph, he'll be all right,' said Nan, 'bit of food, make sure he's warm at night, that's all he needs.' Nan loved birds. No one was allowed to say a word against her bantam hens, and even when her favourite pink-and-grey galah bit off half the top of Jill's finger, it was Jill's fault, not cocky's.

I devised my own method of feeding Muddy. I simply placed a small piece of meat on the end of my finger and then stuck it down his throat. The technique seemed to suit him; in no time at all, he'd grown into a fine, healthy bird. I was his mother and he was my pal, and while our greatest adventure together was no more than running errands to the corner shop, in my mind we experienced far more exciting escapades. About that time, I was into reading the 'Famous Five' books; Muddy fulfilled the role of Timmy, George's dog.

At night, Mud slept on a chair in my room. Jill didn't like him much. 'Don't put him next to my bed, he might poop on me.' She flung herself under the rugs, leaving me to study her lumpy figure in resentment.

I wondered if I could make him poop on her. I glanced at Mud, perched in his usual place, his feet entwined around the chair back next to my bed. Better not encourage him, I decided, Mum would never forgive me. I yawned and snuggled down. 'Night, Mud,' I whispered. He stared back, his eyes intense. I often wished birds could talk. I was considering trying to teach Mud some sign language. My eyes grew heavy and gradually closed. Mud raised his left claw twice. Yes! Twice for yes and once for no! I knew he could do it. That night, I dreamt of all the tricks I would teach him. What a show that would be: Mud and me, stars!

The next morning, I awoke to silence, I yawned and stretched. Normally, Muddy's shrill, hungry calls disturbed my sleep; this morning, there were none. I glanced at his chair, Mud was hanging upside-down. I half-smiled. Must be a new trick, I thought.

'Birds just don't do tricks like that, dear,' Mum explained

to me later.

I felt terrible. Mud had hung stiffly upside-down, not because he was concentrating on a new trick, but because rigor mortis had set in.

He joined a host of past pets buried under the fig tree in the far corner of our yard. Now, when I ran errands to the corner shop, no one commented on the wild mudlark perched precariously on my shoulder. There was just me, a scrawny, pigtailed kid wearing grubby clothes and a sulky look. Adventures, even in your imagination, were no fun on your own.

9

CURE-ALLS

The swamp behind our place had become an important place for me. It was now part of me, part of what I was as a person. When I was in the swamp, I lost all track of time. I wallowed in the small brown creek that meandered through on its way to join the Canning River. I caught gilgies by hanging over an old stormwater drain and wriggling my fingers in the water. As soon as the gilgies latched on, it required only a quick flick of the wrist to land them, gasping, on the bank. I imagined myself an adventurer, always curious to know what was around the next bend, or behind the clump of taller gums I glimpsed in the distance.

I loved to think of the swamp as a very wild place. Every summer, our neighbours caught at least three or four large dugites and tiger snakes. It was strange, in all my forays into the bush, I never encountered any. I sensed they were about, but as long as I stayed out of their way, they seemed happy to stay out of mine.

Jill and I had many fun times down there. And we were always carting home some new find to show Nan. Once she'd inspected our prizes and we'd discussed what they were and how they lived, she'd make us return them to the swamp.

There was no need to visit the swamp during winter, because our backyard invariably flooded with water teeming with tadpoles and small fish. Normally, the water rose to just above our ankles, but after a really good rain, it would get as high as halfway up our lower legs. Such days were greeted with squeals of delight as we splashed about, squeezing our toes into the muddy bottom and flicking up sand at one another.

Nan's view of the physical world was a deeply personal one. When she wasn't outside chopping wood or raking leaves, she was observing the weather. Her concern with atmospheric conditions was based on a rather pessimistic view of the frequency of natural disasters. Even though she listened avidly to weather reports on the radio, she never put complete faith in any meteorologist's opinion. Nan knew their predictions weren't as reliable as her own.

Daily, she checked the sky, the clouds, the wind, and, on particularly still days, the reactions of our animals. Sometimes, she would sit up half the night, checking on the movement of a particular star, or pondering the meaning of a new colour she'd seen in the sky at sunset.

On rare occasions, Mum was called in for consultation. It always amused me to see them standing at the end of our footpath, arms raised upwards, as if in supplication — Nan pointing out various dubious cumulus formations, and Mum nodding and muttering, 'Yes, yes. I see what you mean.' Then they would both test the wind direction with a wet finger. Nan's catchphrase at such times was, 'You never know, Glad. You just never know what the weather could bring.'

Since Dad had died, Nan had developed various emergency routines to cope with what she considered likely natural disasters. For earthquakes, she instructed us to run onto the oval opposite our house, avoiding the electric light poles as we went. If we were unfortunate enough to have the earth open up in front of us, we had to jump as high as we could, and hope that by the time we came down, the earth would have closed up again. While the threat of a major quake was considered extremely remote by the rest of our neighbourhood, Nan had convinced us that it was one of the hazards of daily living. I used to have nightmares where I'd picture myself running onto the oval in my pyjamas as electric light poles crashed and thundered around me.

Besides earthquakes, Nan feared storms. Lightning and thunder, her old favourites, never failed to trigger her panic button. Tearing through the house like a whirlwind, she swept us up in her arms and deposited us in a jumbled heap in the hall. Then she raced to the back verandah and dragged in a box of firewood. Hurrying back, she thrust a large, splintery piece of wood into each pair of reluctant hands, with the cryptic instruction, 'Don't you kids let go of those or you'll get electrocuted.'

We were so frightened we didn't dare move. While we sat on the floor, Nan hurried from room to room, switching off lights and throwing sheets over mirrors, crockery, cutlery, the bath and even the kitchen sink. Once this was done, she dashed to the meter-box and pulled out all the fuses.

In Nan's mind, lightning and electricity were one and the same, both dangerous and totally untrustworthy. She removed the fuses because that meant the electricity, inspired by the raging storm, couldn't escape and harm us. She threw sheets and blankets over anything shiny because it was common knowledge there was nothing lightning loved better than a shiny surface.

If we were lucky, the storm soon passed, but there were occasions when we sat on the floor all afternoon, clutching our chunks of firewood.

'Can't we get up now?'

'You just sit still,' Nan said tersely, glowering over us as she guarded the door to the kitchen in case one of us should make a bid for freedom. 'You kids don't know what storms are. I've seen them up North. Terrible, terrible things. People have been killed.'

When Mum returned from work, we would still be sitting there, our limbs numb with cold.

'Oh get up, you kids,' Mum said in exasperation as she

threw Nan a disgusted look.

Mum lit the fire and Nan stormed off to her room in a fit of rage.

By tea-time, Nan had cooled down. She would emerge, grumpily, from her room and begin to peel potatoes. We knew then everything was back to normal.

Almost a year to the day after Dad died, I contracted rheumatic fever. Many times on the way to school, I had to stop and hold my chest until the pain had passed. Mum rushed me to the doctor twice, but he maintained that I was merely suffering from growing pains. I had no idea that getting taller could be such agony.

Nights were the worst. I curled myself up into a tight little ball and willed the pain to go away. I hurt too much to cry. Nan tried to help me as much as she could. I could tell she was worried about me. She admonished me for sleeping in such a peculiar position and then, gently, she straightened out my arms and legs. I remember a couple of nights, when I was particularly bad, she just ran her hands slowly down the full length of my body, not touching me, but saying, 'You'll be all right, I won't let anything happen to you.'

I learnt a valuable lesson from being so sick, I learnt I was strong inside. I had to be to survive. Eventually my illness subsided without any medical treatment.

Nan had many beliefs to do with health that she passed on to us. She was obsessed with healthy bowels. So was Mum. Nan worried about people who stayed in the toilet too long. If Mum took longer than ten minutes, Nan manifested her concern by knocking on the door and calling, 'Glad...are you in there?'

I later realised that the time Mum spent in the toilet was her only chance for peace and quiet. With five children in the house, where else could she go?

Both Mum and Nan convinced us that a lot of illness was caused by constipation. We were quite happy to go along with their views in theory, but when their obsession began to extend to us in the form of regular doses of castor oil,

Laxettes and what we crudely termed 'glycerine sticks', we balked. Our co-operation became more and more difficult to obtain, and Mum finally decided that the hassle in first discovering our separate hiding-places and then literally dragging us from them wasn't worth the satisfaction she got when we all lined up for the toilet.

In a sense, Mum and Nan weren't health fanatics so much as sickness fanatics. They took great pleasure in reading about diseases with unknown causes. They were particularly interested in tropical medicine, reasoning that as Australia was within cooee of the equator, anything could come wafting down. We were convinced that leprosy and the bubonic plague abounded in our piece of suburbia, and when we caught measles and chicken-pox, we wondered what they would lead to. Nan also convinced me that most doctors were untrustworthy. For years, she had been talking about the Old Cures, the ones they used in the early days.

One of Nan's great cure-alls was pepper. Any gashes were stuffed full with pepper and then tightly bound with strips torn from an old sheet. She also believed that eating a tin of beetroot would replace the blood you lost. While we exhibited various higgledy-piggledy scars on our arms and legs, the result of wounds stitched at Hollywood Repatriation Hospital, Nan had none. Her skin always healed soft and whole.

Two of Nan's health measures I found difficult to accept. The first concerned Enos. She regularly dosed herself with Enos because she was convinced it helped oxygenate the blood. 'You try it, Sally,' she said to me one day. 'It makes your blood clean and your head clear.' I did take a mouthful, but I immediately spat it out.

The second involved kerosene. Nan maintained it was wonderful for removing aches and pains and for generally keeping your body in tiptop condition. When I was suffering from rheumatic fever, Nan begged me to let her rub my arms and legs with it. I steadfastly refused; I hated the smell. Nan was so conscientious about her twice-daily kerosene rubs we feared that, combined with her chain-smoking, a sudden blaze might one day be the cause of her death.

Nan's interest in health was not restricted to the human population.

One hot Saturday afternoon, when I was stretched out on a towel soaking up the sun, it slowly dawned on my numbed senses that Nan's restless movements around the yard had ceased. I took a quick glance around to see where she was.

She was standing very still, close to the smallest gum tree in our backyard. Using the back of her knuckles, she tapped the trunk twice, and then once with her stick. Then she inclined her head towards the trunk as though listening for something. After a lengthy pause she seemed satisfied, and, giving the earth a quick prod with her stick, she moved on to the paperbark.

'Nan,' I called out, 'what on earth are you doing?'

She started in surprise. I had been quiet for so long it was obvious she'd forgotten I was there. She waved her stick at me in a threatening manner and said crossly, 'I'm not doing anything, you go back to sleep!'

'Come on, Nan, I saw you tapping on that tree, what were you doing?'

She jabbed her stick in the sand, turned to me and said, 'I can't walk round my own backyard without one of you kids spying on me.'

'I just happened to see what you were doing, that's all. Now, are you going to tell me or not?'

She could see I wasn't going to give up without a fight, so she said quickly: 'I was just checking on them to make sure they were all right, that's all. Now, no more questions, I got work to do!'

'Okay,' I sighed as I burrowed my head down into my towel once again.

What on earth did she mean, making sure they were all right? I puzzled over her words for a few seconds, then dismissed them. There was so much about Nan I didn't understand.

10

GETTING AHEAD

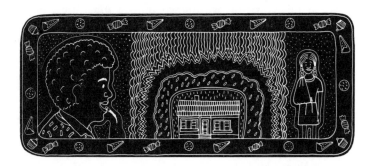

The year I started Grade Six, Mum was offered a job as a cleaner at our school. The hours were perfect, because they fitted in with the two other part-time jobs she was doing. But she didn't accept the job straight away. First, she got us all together and asked if we would mind her taking it.

'What on earth are you talking about, Mum?' I said.

'Well, I don't want to take the job if you children would mind. I thought you might worry about what your friends would think.'

Without hesitation I replied, 'We wouldn't mind, Mum, we'd really like it because we'd see more of you.'

Mum smiled at me. She knew I didn't realise that being a school cleaner carried very little status.

We helped after school, wiping down the boards, emptying the bins and sweeping the floors. I enjoyed the boards the most, mainly because it gave me access to the chalk. Before wiping them down, I would scrawl rude comments about school across the whole length of the wall. It gave me a great sense of power.

With more money coming in, Mum took to indulging us whenever she could. This indulgence took the form of unlimited lollies and fruit, rather than new clothes, toys or books. She'd managed to take us all to the Royal Show the year before; this year, because of her new job, she told us we would really do it in style.

Like the year before, our first port of call was our uncle's amusement centre in sideshow alley. We thought it was a magical place. While we looked at the machines, Mum chattered on to Uncle, discussing one triviality after another. Even when Uncle excused himself on the pretext of fixing one of his money-grabbing machines, Mum followed, mentioning the weather or some person they both knew. Eventually, Uncle fished out five ten-bob notes and told us all to run along. Mum could be boring when it suited her.

We bought show-bags crammed with Smarties, Cherry Ripes, Samboy Potato Chips and Violet Crumble bars. We weren't interested in the educational ones. Mum insisted on buying Nan a Mills and Ware suitcase filled with biscuits. Nan loved it. She ate all the biscuits then used the suitcase to store things in.

One of our show-bags had a packet of marshmallows in it and Mum came up with the super idea of toasting them over the fire. Just like the Famous Five! We were all terribly excited about this, we loved anything new.

While Mum stoked up the fire, we all gathered sticks from the garden. I cleaned down my stick as best I could, then hurriedly shoved a marshmallow on the end and placed it close to the coals. It immediately smoked and went black. Everyone laughed. Jill insisted on having a turn, but the same thing happened. Finally, Mum squeezed between us, her stick adorned with blobs of pink and white, one marshmallow for each of us.

We waited patiently. Mum'll be able to do it, we thought. She can do anything when she sets her mind to it. Seconds passed. We all leapt up in fright when she let out a sudden shriek.

'Arrgh! Stupid thing!' Dropping her stick, she jumped up, holding her hand. The bottom pink marshmallow, closest to the coals, had melted quicker than the others and slid down onto her hand. It was hot and sticky, and clung tightly as Mum tried to remove it by stretching it from one hand to the other.

We all choked. Mum's pantomime had us in stitches. The stick she'd dropped had fallen into the fire, and the remaining marshmallows were smoking vigorously. Carefully, I reached over and flicked her stick from the fire with my own. It lay on the floorboards, blackened and sticky. Mum retreated to the kitchen, and fifteen minutes later returned with a tray laden with tea, toast and jam, and sardines. Soon we were all laughing and joking as we normally did on a Sunday night.

For Nan, Mum's extra job meant she had more work to do around the house, but it also meant a reasonable amount to bet on the TAB. Sometimes Nan let us pick a horse, too, and she would get the lady next door to lay a bet for us as well. We had a rule in our house when it came to backing horses: never back the same horse as Nan, they never came in. Before any of us picked our horses, we asked Nan which ones she fancied. It narrowed the field down considerably.

Besides the TAB, Nan loved lottery tickets. Both she and Mum were convinced that one day our family would come into a lot of money. It was a poor man's dream, but we believed it. The dream became such a reality in my mind that I often thought, well, it doesn't matter if I don't get a job when I'm grown up, we'll probably have won the lottery by then. Billy thought the same. Jill was the only one among us who seemed keen to work at anything.

Having more money also meant that Nan could indulge in chain-smoking. In fact, she took to smoking so consistently that the front of her hair changed colour. While the rest of her frizzy mop was a light grey, the front was nicotine-yellow. When we pointed it out to her she was quite pleased. 'It's better than hair dye,' she chuckled as she looked in the mirror. 'Now if only I could get it to go round the back as well...' She had mastered the skill of being able to talk and smoke at the same time. It seemed it didn't matter what Nan did, her cigarette remained glued to the corner of her mouth. However while smoking, and the cough she was developing with it, were an integral part of her personality, there were two important occasions when she didn't smoke.

For a long time, one of her greatest pleasures had been to lie in bed at night and enjoy a leisurely puff. But one night she'd set fire to her mattress. Mum, seeing the smoke, had rushed in and thrown a kettle of water over her. Nan hated getting wet, so she gave up her night-time fag.

The other occasion was during summer when the dry bush surrounding the swamp would ignite into a raging bushfire. She never smoked then. She felt it added to the heat.

Bushfires were a real threat to our house in those days. As billowing clouds of black smoke engulfed the neighbourhood, the firemen came knocking at each door with the message: 'Look luv, if the wind doesn't change soon, you'll have to evacuate.'

Nan always responded with: 'We're not leavin', this is the only home we got.' If the men tried to argue with her, she pointed to her garden hose and said, 'You're not the only ones with water, you know.'

Their usual response to that was to try to explain how easily the flames could leap from roof to roof. Nan countered this by giving them a tour of our yard just to show them how many hoses she had. For some reason, six strategically placed garden hoses meant little to the firemen. 'Listen, luv,' they reasoned, 'if that wind doesn't change, the flames'll be in next door's and then they'll be in your place and you'll all go up in smoke. You got five kids here, too, can't someone have them for the day?'

'We got no one,' Nan would reply grumpily. 'Anyway, they're all right, I've wet them down.' It was true, we were dripping wet. Any hint of a fire in the swamp and Nan would line us all up and squirt us down with the hose. Then it was the chooks', cats', dogs' and budgies' turn.

Sometimes, Mum thought Nan's precautions were a little premature. 'Goodness, have you wet them down already?'

she'd complain. 'No one's even called the Fire Brigade yet!' Nan always narrowed her eyes and looked at Mum as though she couldn't believe how stupid she was. When Mum turned to go inside, she'd squirt her with the hose.

Nan kept great stores of men's handkerchiefs in case of fire. She would wet them, then plaster them over our heads and faces. It made it easier to breathe when the ash rained down.

Fortunately for us, the wind always did change, and we survived the heat, ash and billowing smoke. It was only when the fire in the swamp was completely out that Nan would relax and light up another cigarette.

Grade Six in primary school wasn't a bad year for me. Jill and I were often taken off normal classwork to help paint and design special things for the school. Also, I liked my teacher. He was firm, but very kind, and he got on well with Mum. He'd broken his nose as a child, so he was an unusual-looking man. I was impressed with the way he joked about his nose and never let its odd shape worry him. He always used to point out to the accident-prone ones in our class how they would end up if they didn't stop doing silly things.

I was unexpectedly made president of the Red Cross Club that year. Part of my job was instructing younger children in road safety. There was also a paper test that they sat for in their lunch hour. If they passed, I was allowed to award them a Safety First Certificate. Jill sat for the test and went home crying because I failed her. You were only allowed to make two errors and she, uncharacteristically, had made three. Mum was furious. She maintained I should have passed Jill simply because we were related. Jill sat the test the following week and passed and I breathed a sigh of relief.

They had a Safety First Week at school that year and several members of parliament were invited to attend. Being president of the Red Cross Club, I was to have the honour of showing them over the class displays. That Friday, just before the bell rang for home time, our teacher warned us again to be careful over the weekend. Unfortunately, our class was accident-prone. There was a small nucleus of children who were always missing the bus for swimming, skinning their knees on the playground, jamming their fingers in sliding doors. We glanced guiltily at one another, each wondering who was going to be stupid enough to muff it.

I was extra careful that weekend, but on Sunday, Billy teased me once too often. I decided to teach him a lesson. Around the house we ran, Billy's howls of laughter slowly changing to cries of trepidation as I gained on him. As we rounded the corner for the fourth time, Billy decided he needed Mum's protection. He leapt onto the front porch, flung open the door and darted inside, slamming the door in my face as he went. I was running so fast I was unable to stop myself from going into it. Unfortunately for me, the entire door, except for the frame, was made of glass. I went straight through and landed with a thud against the inside wall. I screamed when I looked down at my arm. There was a large slice of skin missing, and a long, pulsating blue vein protruding.

Mum came running. She took one look at the multitude of tiny cuts all over my body, then focused on the gash in my arm and shrieked, 'Oh, my God!' Wrapping my arm in a towel, she drove straight to Hollywood Hospital. On arrival, they placed us both on stretchers and, while they stitched me up, Mum revived. A cup of tea and two Milk Arrowroot biscuits later and she was her old self.

On Monday, I arrived at school with a large white sling, an armful of stitches and a guilty conscience. My teacher eyed me in dismay. I conducted the tour of the Safety Displays anyway, trying to walk discreetly, with the injured part of my body turned away from our Very Important Guests. I think they found my efforts amusing.

That Christmas, Mum's old friend Lois gave her a dog, a tiny pedigree terrier. When Billy first heard we were getting another dog, he was keen for it to be his. He was sick of family pets. However, when he saw the size of it, he changed his mind. What self-respecting eight-year-old boy would want to be seen with a dog that size yapping at his heels?

But Jill loved our new dog and her affection was returned. Tiger, as she named him, soon answered only to her. Tiger used to yap viciously from our bedroom window-sill every morning at anything that moved. I complained to Mum one morning that she never let him outside. It wasn't a healthy way for a dog to live. Mum said she was afraid he might get run over or bite someone. I howled with laughter.

But, partly because Tiger spent his time tearing around the house destroying anything he could sink his fangs into, Mum relented. Tiger was given his freedom and then proceeded to attack the car next door. By the time Mum managed to catch him, she was worn to a frazzle.

We were certainly glad Widdles wasn't fierce. He'd grown into a beautiful big dog and could have really hurt someone if that was his nature. With absolutely no encouragement on our part, he'd trained himself to do helpful things around the house, like bringing in the paper and generally tidying up the place. He shared his food and bed with our black-and-white cat and had never been in trouble in his life.

Tiger decided that he liked his freedom, so as soon as Mum opened the front door early in the morning, he darted swiftly between her legs and tore onto the oval opposite. There was a large group of neighbourhood dogs who were in the habit of taking an early morning stroll; Tiger loved to nip behind each one and sink his sharp little fangs into their back legs. Within minutes, the pack would be in a frenzy and Mum would dispatch faithful old Widdles to the rescue. He would bark his authority over the pack, then pick Tiger up by the scruff of the neck and carry him home.

It was a wonderful partnership, but one destined for an early end.

One afternoon, Mum broke the sad news to Jill that Tiger had passed on. Jill naturally assumed that one of the bigger dogs from the pack had finally got its revenge. Mum found it difficult to keep a straight face as she explained how Tiger had single-handedly attacked the number thirty-seven bus.

It was a fitting end.

With all Mum's extra jobs, the money was really rolling in. At least, that's how it seemed to us. For one thing, we now had access to quantities of food, especially during winter. We arrived home from school soaked to the skin, dumped our bags in the hall, then made straight for the wood stove in the kitchen, where we set our smelly shoes and socks to dry on the open door of the oven. I always managed to squeeze closest to the fire, and, when Nan wasn't looking, I poked my bare feet inside the oven, a practice that invariably led to chilblains.

'Eat! Eat!' Nan commanded as she placed huge chunks of jam tart and mince pie before us. 'You kids got to eat. I know what it's like to be hungry, it's a terrible thing.'

We never thought much about the way Nan carried on over food, never considered the possibility that she might have known hard times. We had no conception of what it was like to have a really empty stomach; even when Dad was alive, there'd always been something to fill up on. Nan had cooked rabbit a lot and she was good at making damper. Now, we had food aplenty, and Nan was giving us the impression that going without food for any length of time wasn't normal. While she thought she was doing the right thing by squeezing in as many meals as possible in one day, it would lead to eating habits later in life that were difficult to break.

We learnt not only to eat in quantity, but quickly as well. It was a matter of expediency. The child who finished its dinner last often had part of its dessert pinched, or missed out on the extra baked potatoes browning in the oven.

Our conversations were never regulated, either. We all spoke at once, and whoever had the loudest voice or the funniest story dominated the table, even if his or her mouth was full of potato.

There was nothing we loved better than huddling around the wood stove on cold afternoons, swapping stories. An open fire was always at the centre of our family gatherings.

If it wasn't inside, it was out in the yard. And if it wasn't the wood stove in the kitchen, it was the red-brick fireplace in the lounge-room. We felt very secure in front of an open fire.

Countless times, after Nan had woken me early to show me something special in the garden, she said, 'Come inside, we'll light the fire.' I screwed up newspaper and Nan pushed the kindling in on top then passed me the matches. I lit it just the way she'd shown me, striking the match away from my body.

Once the fire was lit, Nan passed me the toasting fork, handmade out of two bits of wire twined together. There were three sharp prongs and a long handle with a loop on the end so you could hang it on a nail next to the stove. The nail had fallen out a couple of years ago and never been replaced, so now we kept it lying around on top of the oven.

I stabbed a piece of sliced white bread and poked it towards the flames. Having singed one side, I quickly turned it over and singed the other. It couldn't really be called toast, because it was soft in the middle, but on cold mornings, topped with melted butter and lashings of jam, it soon warmed an empty tummy. By the time the kettle boiled, we'd eaten at least six slices.

Pretty soon, my four brothers and sisters wandered out and demanded breakfast. 'What's for brekky?' Jill slurred as she eyed me gulping the last sweet, sticky remnants of tea in my mug. 'S'pose you've eaten all the toast.'

'Get a move on, Sally,' Nan muttered. 'You get dressed for school and let Jilly cook the toast now.' I was always reluctant to leave the warmth of the fire. Slowly I eased myself off the small white stool and let Jill take my place. I knew she hated cooking toast. She was a puzzle to me, she didn't like gutting chickens or chopping wood, either, and she kept her clothes neat and tidy. She had a natural sense of order.

11

TRIUMPHS AND FAILURES

Grade Seven was a mixture of triumphs and failures. It was also the year my brother David began primary school.

David was a quiet, gentle little boy with lots of imagination. Unfortunately for him, he was landed with a teacher who was a middle-aged spinster, stern and unyielding. David was easily flustered, especially when he was trying to do the right thing; he was continually in trouble over minor details like lost rubbers, books and pencils. It wasn't, of course, entirely David's fault; our home was so disorganised it was difficult to find large items, let alone the small things he was supposed to keep in his school case.

David seemed to spend most of his first year at school crying over the recurring loss of his black print pencil. We knew that whenever he burst into tears at home, the first words to come from his wobbly mouth would be 'Black Print Pencil!'

Mum was disgusted at the hard attitude his teacher seemed to be taking towards him. She bought David a couple of extra black print pencils as back-ups. However, David was so absent-minded that he soon lost track of those as well. I lost count of the number of times he ran from the lower end of our primary school to the upper end, where Jill and I had to console him over his latest disaster. Invariably, it was the dreaded Black Print Pencil.

In that last year at primary school, I developed an allergy to chalk. On one of my many trips to the doctor, Mum naively inquired, 'Do you think it's the chalk, doctor? She seems to get an attack of hay fever every time she goes near the blackboard.'

I was amazed that, by now, Mum hadn't twigged to the fact that I was allergic to school, not chalk. To my even greater amusement, the doctor prevaricated; he was filling in for our family doctor and it was his first year out of the hospital. He'd never heard of it happening, but then, anything was possible.

The chalk allergy proved a wonderful bonus. I no longer lingered over breakfast or dragged my feet reluctantly down the footpath when it was time to leave for school. Instead, I walked off cheerfully, secure in the knowledge that by midmorning I would be on my way home again.

At the beginning of third term I won the coveted Dick Cleaver Award for Citizenship. The whole school voted. I wondered who Jill had bribed — she had a lot of influence in the lower grades. My prize was a choice of any book available from the bookshops. When our headmaster, Mr Buddee, asked me what I had in mind, I replied, without hesitation, 'A book of fairy tales, please.' I think he was rather taken aback, because he told me to go away and think about it for a few days. I stuck to my choice, even though my class teacher tried to talk me into something more suitable. My class-mates thought I was potty, too. They didn't understand. I knew fairy tales were the stuff dreams were made of. And I loved dreams.

Mr Buddee announced to the school assembly one morning that our end-of-year extravaganza was going to be the biggest we'd ever had. We were all excited, especially when we heard there would be dancing and play-acting as well as singing and exhibitions of our work. He was a very creative man.

I was convinced that because of my inability to co-ordinate my limbs, I wouldn't be chosen for anything, and I desperately wanted to participate in one of the dances. So my glee knew no bounds when my teacher informed me that I was to be in the Dance of the Black Swans, as well as the Maypole. Jill was also very excited, because she was chosen for the Dance of the Leaves.

In no time at all, it seemed, the big night was upon us. To the sound of the pianola, thirty pairs of painted black swan feet swept onto the bitumen playground. We held our heads stiffly and our arms and legs flowed in unison, gliding as a swan might across a lake. A host of adoring Mums and Dads, all of whom thought their particular daughter a budding Margot Fonteyn, watched proudly. All, of course, except my Mum. She cherished many illusions, but that wasn't one of them.

With the applause for the Black Swan Dance still ringing in my ears, I waited with baited breath to participate in the Maypole. My over-confidence was to be my undoing. Half-way through the second time around, I suddenly realised my red ribbon was pulling on the other girls', and the girl normally ahead of me was now two places behind. I couldn't understand what had happened. Hadn't I woven an intricate pattern in a graceful and gentle manner? I looked up: to my dismay, I realised I had indeed woven a pattern, so intricate no one had been able to follow it. The hushed whispers from the audience were not from admiration but embarrassment.

Dropping my tightly held red ribbon, I pushed past the other girls and fled. I could still hear the music playing as I hid in shame behind one of the darkened class-rooms. I prayed the earth would open and swallow me up so I wouldn't have to face my class-mates. The music finally ended, and I heard Mrs Oldfield, our Maypole teacher, thunder past growling, 'Where is that girl?' I was stricken with terror.

After about half an hour Mum found me. 'Don't be silly,

Sally,' she scolded as she looked down at my huddled form. She bundled me into the car and we drove home in silence. Jill held her sides and stared out of the window all the way. Mum had forbidden her to laugh.

During that final year, I noticed that whenever we brought our friends home to play after school, Nan would disappear.

'How come Nan nicks off when our friends are here?' I asked Jill one day.

'Dunno. She's been doin' it for years.'

'I never noticed.'

'You never notice anything!'

Later that day, I asked Mum the same question. She put it down to Nan's old age. In my mind, Nan had always been old. I couldn't imagine her actually getting older, though. She was the sort of person that would stay the same age for ever.

One day, I walked into the kitchen with one of my friends and there was Nan making a cup of tea. She was furious with me. After my friend had left she said, 'You're not to keep bringin' people inside, Sally. You got no shame. We don't want them to see how we live.'

'Why not?'

'People talk. We don't want people talkin' about us. You dunno what they might say!'

'Okay, Nan,' I agreed. It wasn't often I had friends after school, I wasn't pally with a lot of kids.

Towards the end of the year our class was given a batch of IQ tests. We were told they were a sure way of measuring our intelligence. The tests would indicate which stream we would be placed in the following year, in high school. There were only two streams: the Professional, which generally included at least two maths and one science subject, and was aimed at entrance to university or other advanced education; and the Commercial, which meant you took shorthand and typing and left school at fifteen. On the basis of the tests, it was recommended I should be placed in the Commercial stream.

Mr Buddee took a personal interest in my case. He couldn't understand how I could do so well in school, despite all my illnesses, yet so badly in the IQ tests. One morning he called Mum in for an interview and explained to her the difficulty he was having in getting me placed in the Professional stream. By the time I was ushered into the office, Mum was sitting next to Mr Buddee with a dumbfounded look on her face. She'd never heard of IQ tests before; I believe she thought they'd discovered I was mentally retarded.

Mr Buddee asked me if I had been ill on the day of the tests. He also asked if there was anything I would like to say about them. I felt incredibly stupid. I wanted to explain my feelings, but whenever anyone questioned me directly about anything, I automatically clammed up.

We had been given one test after another. There were pages of complicated drawings and numerous questions about farmers and their produce. It wasn't long before I came to regard Farmer Jones and his three sons, with their two bushels of wheat, five bags of navel oranges and three tons of granny smiths, as cretins. When I wasn't daydreaming, I simply marked each multiple choice question a,b,c simultaneously.

That night, I pestered Mum to tell me what Mr Buddee had said. At first she refused, but finally explained what it all meant. I was deeply offended by the fact that I had been labelled dumb by the stupid, boring test. Yet I was excited by the prospect that I would be allowed to leave school at fifteen. Mum wasn't having a bar of it. She was determined that, by hook or by crook, I would go on to tertiary studies.

'But Mum, the only place I want to study is at that famous art school in Paris. If I can't do that, I don't care what I do.'

Mum was aghast. She protested that she wasn't made of money. 'Wouldn't you miss your family?' she added as an afterthought.

'Naah,' I retorted, 'I'd be too busy painting.'

Poor Mum. I gave her the run-around for years. She deserved better.

12

GROWING UP

The summer following my final year in primary school signalled the start of my growing up. I was very self-conscious. None of my body seemed to be in proportion. I had long legs, long arms and the bit in between was flat and skinny. I think what I disliked most about myself, though, was the lack of pigmentation in certain patches of skin around my neck and shoulders. I always buttoned my shirts right up to the collar. If the top button was missing, I pulled my collar close in around my neck and held it there with a large safety-pin.

Mum must have noticed, because she took me to see a skin specialist, who said there was nothing he could do and referred me to a cosmetician, and I was given make-up to mix together to conceal my patches.

After all the trouble Mum had gone to, I didn't have the courage to tell her I had no intention of using the make-up. Actually, I was mad at her. It was one thing for me to stick a safety-pin in my collar, quite another for her to drag me around to specialists, exhibiting me to the world. I threw my make-up in the bin. It was a symbolic gesture. I decided that from then on I would bare that part of my body. If people were repulsed, that was their problem, not mine. It was the first time my lower neck had seen the light of day for months.

Apart from my appearance, my main worry was high school. For a time, I had romantic notions about running away to join a circus. I would climb into the small gum tree in our backyard and sit there for hours, day-dreaming about circus life. But the circus never came and, in February 1964, I started high school.

I felt terribly old-fashioned. I still had two long plaits dangling down my back. All the other girls had short hair, and were much more mature than me. There were about twelve hundred students. I felt lost and intimidated.

As we all waited silently in line that first day, I kept wondering which stream they were going to put me in, Commercial or Professional. We'd been told there were four Professional classes, denoted by the letters A to D. Only the exceptionally brainy students were permitted in the A class. I sat glumly as the teachers read through the A list, the B and C. By the time they got to the bottom of the D list my name still hadn't been mentioned. Suddenly the principal came over and joined our group. After a brief conversation with one of the teachers he called out, 'Is there a Sally Milroy here?'

Slowly I raised my hand.

'You're in D group, too, off you go,' he said. I didn't know whether I wanted to laugh or cry. I hated school, yet, at the same time, I didn't want people thinking I was the sort of kid who didn't have a brain in her head.

Mum was ecstatic when I arrived home. Apparently Mr Buddee had told her he'd fixed things up. She greeted me excitedly. 'Maybe you'll become a vet now!' That seemed the next best thing to being a doctor.

'I've gone off animals, Mum,' I replied sarcastically.

'A doctor, then?' Mum said hopefully.

'Don't like 'em.'

'Well, anything Sally, anything. You've got too much talent to waste.'

'Look, Mum,' I said, 'can I have something to eat? I'm starving.'

'Jam tart in here,' Nan called from the kitchen. 'Leave the child alone, Glad. She's got to eat.'

Mum was rather deflated. I think she expected me to be as excited as she was. As I sat munching a huge piece of jam tart, I found myself feeling a little sorry for her. She had five kids and she seemed to be pinning her hopes on me, the worst one. Jill would be the one to achieve something, not me. I sighed and cut myself another slice. There were four kids in our family younger than me — at least one of them must have a good chance of becoming a doctor, especially if Mum kept pushing. I didn't like to think of all of us ending up as failures.

Early in the school year I made friends with a girl called Steph. She lived seven blocks away from us in the part of our suburb they called Como, and we took to visiting each other on weekends. I was fascinated by Steph's family, they were very neat and tidy. I loved Steph's bedroom, it was decorated mainly in lilac and reminded me of something straight out of a Hollywood film set. Surprisingly, Steph was equally fascinated by my home. She loved the free-and-easy atmosphere, and the tall stories and jokes.

I think my intense admiration for Steph's room caused me to become somewhat dissatisfied. I suddenly realised there was a whole world beyond what I knew. It was frightening. Sometimes, when Steph's parents talked to me, my mind went blank. I always seemed to say the wrong thing, so, for fear of offending them, I began saying nothing at all, which was even worse.

That year, Mr Willie took us to the usual Legacy march. It was our fourth since Dad had died and I still disliked them. When I told kids at school I'd be marching for Legacy, they all killed themselves laughing. 'Talk about daggy,' one of them muttered. I desperately wanted to be like them, but I just didn't seem to be made of the right stuff.

Even my attempt at a new hairdo failed. Mum had been

adamant in her refusal to allow me to go to the hairdresser, so in desperation, I simply chopped off my two plaits, leaving stubby, half-plaited wads of hair. Mum was so embarrassed that she took me up the road to the local lady who did hairdressing from home. Her efforts weren't much better than mine, but at least my hair was now even. Nan was the only one who had anything good to say. ''Minds me of the old days, seein' you like that, Sally,' she said chirpily. 'That's what they call a basin-cut.'

I tried everything I could to get out of marching that year, but Mum enlisted the help of Mr Willie. I could never resist his 'Your Father Was A Brave Man' routine. As a reward for my capitulation, Mum said I could wear Dad's big medals, while Bill wore the miniatures. Jill sported a couple of medals from World War One that belonged to somebody else.

Mr Willie gave us a special treat that year, morning tea in his office at the top of the AMP building. It was the tallest building in Perth in those days and we were anxious to see the view. As it turned out, we were more impressed with Mr Willie's office than the view. It was spacious, with soft carpet and an imposing desk, but what fascinated us most of all was his little fridge. To begin with, when you opened the door, it lit up. Ours never did. It was packed with cool drinks and cake, and we were amazed to discover that it was for his use only. None of us said anything, but we all looked at each other as if to say, so this is how wealthy people live, you all have your own personal fridge.

Towards the middle of that year Nan and I had our first major row. I arrived home from school one day with the facts from a science lesson freshly imprinted in my mind, and proceeded to inform Nan that when it came to eradicating germs, onions were totally useless. For years, she had been using freshly chopped onions to sterilise our house. This was the first time I'd ever openly criticised any of her theories concerning our health.

Nan was cross; she said high school had gone to my head,

and accused me of being as silly as my mother. I pointed out that none of my friends ever got sick and they lived without the stink of mouldy onions. Nan retaliated by asserting that one day they'd probably all fall down dead, then they'd wish they'd known about onions.

I walked into my room, flung back the curtains and collected up all the onion quarters that sat neatly along my bedroom window-sill. I hesitated at picking up two of them. They were slightly mouldy and looked at me as if to say, remove us and you'll get a deadly disease, just like your Grandmother says! I grasped them courageously with my bare hands and flung them dramatically in the kitchen bin. 'No more onions,' I told Nan quietly but firmly. I was trying to be rational about the whole thing. After all, I was studying science.

By the time Mum arrived home, we were at it again. Nan knew just how to provoke me. Didn't I realise that I was putting the lives of my brothers and sisters at risk? How else could we maintain a germ-free environment? Mum just stood and watched us in amazement. Nan began to explain what it was all about. I stormed back into my room and screamed, 'I don't care what you say, Mum, no onions. Steph's room doesn't stink the way mine does.'

Mum came and stood in the doorway of my bedroom and eyed me sympathetically. Nan came up behind her and held up a fistful of freshly cut onions, just to annoy me. 'Here they come, Sally,' she growled, 'I'm bringing them in!'

'MUM!' I screamed.

'Well, perhaps you should leave it for now, Nan,' Mum suggested, tactfully.

For the next few days, my room remained onion-free. Then one day, as I lay on my bed, a strong oniony smell came wafting through. I checked my window-sill: nothing there. Suddenly, out of the corner of my eye, I saw some small, curved white objects jutting over the top of my wardrobe. I grabbed the broom from the kitchen and knocked them down.

I ranted and raved at Nan over this latest intrusion, but

she just chuckled and continued to puff on her cigarette.

The following week, she resorted to tucking the onions in the drawer where I kept my underpants. Even Mum thought that was funny. 'You wait until she tucks onions in your corsets,' I grumbled, 'then you won't be laughing.'

'Keep your voice down, Sally,' Mum said, horrified. 'She might hear you. Don't go giving her any more ideas!'

Our battle remained unresolved for the next few weeks, until Nan discovered a product called Medic, which had a very strong, hospital-type odour. It came in a small blue spray-can and was specifically for use with people suffering from colds and flu.

'What a marvellous clean smell that has, Glad,' Nan commented as Mum sprayed a small amount in the kitchen.

'I thought you might like it.' Mum smiled. 'That's why I bought it, you know what that smoker's cough of yours is like. This will help you breathe.'

'Aah, that's good, Glad,' said Nan, inhaling deeply. 'I can feel it clearing my lungs.' Nan thumped her chest with her fist. 'By gee, I feel good now. That's a good medicine, smells like it's got some of the old cures in it. It's not often you get a medicine like that these days.'

From then on, my room smelled of Medic. My clothes and my rugs smelled of Medic. Nan sprayed Medic down the toilet and in the bathroom. The whole house smelled of Medic. I disliked the smell, but it was better than onions.

By the time I turned fourteen and was in second year high school, I was becoming more and more aware that I was different to the other kids at school. I had little in common with the girls in my class. Even Steph was changing. She no longer raced me to the top of the tree in her yard, and she thought my frequent absences from school were something to be ashamed of.

Jill was in high school now, and, as I expected, was having no difficulty at all in fitting in. Sometimes I desperately wished I could be more like her. Everything seemed so hard for me. Even little Helen had taken to school like a duck to water — she began primary school that year.

'Maybe *she'll* be the doctor,' I said sarcastically.

'Yes, perhaps you're right,' Mum replied thoughtfully. 'I'm sure you'll all do well, once you set your minds to it.'

'Setting your mind to it — that's the hard part.'

'You could do anything, if you really wanted to.'

'That's just it, Mum, I don't want to.'

When I looked at other people, I realised how abnormal I was — at least, that's how I felt. None of my brothers and sisters seemed tormented by the things that tormented me. I really felt as though I just couldn't understand the world any more. It was horrible being a teenager.

Part of the reason I hated school was the regimentation. I hated routine. I wanted to do something exciting and different all the time. I really couldn't see the point in learning about subjects I wasn't interested in. I had no long-term goals and my short-term one was to leave school as soon as I could.

I found that the only way to cope was to play truant as much as possible. Being away from school gave me time to think and relieved the pressure. I always felt better inside. I was becoming an expert in ways to miss school. One way was deliberately to miss the school bus that pulled up in front of our local library. I would walk to the stop with Jill, then, when she was talking to her friends, nick off and hide behind the library building. After the bus had pulled in, collected its passengers and left, I would reappear and walk happily home. My excuse to Mum was that the bus was too crowded to fit me on. For some reason, she either believed me or just accepted it.

But one morning, Jill decided she and her friends would truant also. I wasn't keen to help. There were too many of them and they'd never done it before. However, Jill was eager for me to show everyone the ropes, so I agreed.

Five of us hid behind the library that morning, and when the bus pulled in, we all had a chuckle. Our smiling faces soon changed to dismay when, instead of driving off, the bus remained parked at our stop. We were soon joined by an older girl, who had walked up to where we were hiding and said crossly, 'You might as well come out. The driver's not going to leave without you.'

Jill's friends were so embarrassed. Trying to truant was the most adventurous thing they had ever done. They were all petrified the story would get back to their parents. At least I didn't have that worry. Reluctantly, we all walked back down to the bus, accompanied by the boos, jeers and laughter of the forty teenagers already seated.

'You all ought to be ashamed of yourselves,' the driver growled as we hopped on. 'I'll be checking behind there every morning from now on.'

As we drove to school, I sighed and looked out of the window at the passing bush. That was the trouble when amateurs were involved, you always got caught. I decided that from then on, I'd only take Jill with me.

It was also reasonably easy to leave school during recess and lunch-time. Our school was enclosed by bush on three sides. Keeping my eye on the teacher on playground duty, I would slowly edge my way towards the bush. Once I was really close, I would turn and run, then squat down behind a tree and wait to see if anyone was coming after me. If the coast was clear, I'd walk the three miles home, sticking to the cover of the bush, away from busy Manning Road. Pretty soon, a few other students caught on to the same idea. Sometimes we'd come across one another in the bush, grin guiltily, then press on, pretending we hadn't seen each other. Now and then, Jill came with me, but in her opinion, the joy of missing school wasn't worth the long walk home.

One time, Jill talked me into allowing her best friend, Robin, to accompany us. I thought this was a bit risky, because Robin's father was the mathematics teacher. Sure enough, the Headmaster happened to be driving along Manning Road that morning, spotted us in the bush, picked us up and took us back to school. Poor Robin copped the worst. 'You, of all girls,' he scolded her. 'We expect it of the Milroys, but not of girls of your calibre.'

The school began enforcing stricter rules in an attempt to

reduce truancy. Mum had been threatened with the Truant Officer many times. To her, this was as bad as having a policeman call. So she began to try to make us stay at school all day. She was in a difficult situation. While she wanted us to have a good education and get on in the world, she was also sympathetic to our claims of being bored, tired or unhappy. I knew it wasn't so much our truancy that upset her, but the fact that now and then we got caught. Getting caught inevitably brought us to the personal attention of the school staff, which meant that she lost face in their eyes. Like most people, I suppose, Mum liked others, especially those who were educated, to think well of her.

She was particularly upset after one visit to our Head. He had shown her three different sets of handwriting, all purporting to be hers, and excusing either Jill or me from school. 'You've got to get yourselves organised,' she told us crossly. 'If you're going to forge notes from me, at least do it in the same style.'

The longer I stayed at school, the more difficult I became and the more reluctant Mum was to support my truanting. She was tired of the Head and the Guidance Officer ringing her up. I sympathised with her. I was sick of visiting the Guidance Officer myself. I felt very much on the defensive; I knew my visits were based on the premise that there was something wrong with me. In my view, this was totally unfounded. Consequently, my interviews tended to be fairly short, mainly due to my lack of response. Mum was finally advised to allow me to leave school early and become a shop assistant.

However, one day Mum actually encouraged Jill and me to miss school. There was a wonderful sale on, and she said that if we could manage to sneak off in the afternoon, she would buy us some new clothes. The day of the sale also happened to be Sports Day, which gave me a brilliant idea. Jill and I were playing softball that afternoon and we had a friend who was a really good hitter. We arranged for Dawn to belt a beauty out over the embankment. Jill and I made sure we were both fielding in that area and when the ball flew over, we dived after it. Racing down the embankment, we grabbed the ball, flung it back, then headed for Mum's car, which was parked in the street nearby.

The following Monday, Mum was called to the Head's office once again, and Jill and I with her. After he had spoken to Mum privately, we were called in.

'This is a most serious matter, girls,' he said sternly, 'I have even considered calling the police in.'

We were stunned. He ordered us to sit down. I sneaked a look at Mum, but she was staring at the opposite wall.

'Now,' he continued, 'I've had a talk with your mother and I appreciate that she has a difficult task raising you without the help of a husband, so I'm prepared to be lenient this time. You're the eldest, Sally, I know I can count on you to be responsible. If you will tell me the name of the young man who picked you and your sister up, nothing more will be said.'

I could feel my eyes grow suddenly large in my face. My mouth began to quiver at the corners and my stomach rippled. I managed to murmur that I had nothing to say.

The Headmistress was then called in and gave Jill and me a talk about how easy it was to besmirch our reputations.

Ten minutes later, Mum was on her way home and we were back in class. I felt quite proud of myself. The Head had applied considerable pressure, and I hadn't cracked. Just like my Dad in the war. He'd been questioned by the Gestapo about his friends and he hadn't let them down. Well, I hadn't let Mum down, either.

13

A BLACK GRANDMOTHER

On 14 February 1966, Australia's currency changed, from pounds, shillings and pence to dollars and cents. According to Mum and Nan, it was a step backwards. 'There's no money like the old money,' Nan maintained, and Mum agreed. They were shocked when they heard that our new money would not have as much silver in it as the old two-shilling, one-shilling, sixpence and threepence.

'It'll go bad, Glad,' said Nan one night, 'you wait and see. You can't make money like that, it'll turn green.'

Then I noticed that Nan had a jar on the kitchen shelf with a handful of two-shilling pieces in it. Towards the end of the week, the jar was overflowing with silver coins. I could contain my curiosity no longer.

'What are you saving up for, Nan?'

'Nothin'! Don't you touch any of that money!'

I cornered Mum in the bath. 'Okay Mum, why is Nan hoarding all that money? You're supposed to hand it over to the bank and get new money.'

'Don't you say anything to anyone about that money, Sally. It's going to be valuable one day, we're saving it for you kids. When it's worth a lot we'll sell it and you kids can have what we make. You might need it by then.'

I went back in the kitchen. 'Mum told me what you're up to,' I told Nan. 'I think it's crazy.'

'Hmph! We don't care what you think, you'll be glad of it in a few years' time. Now you listen, if anyone from the government comes round asking for money, you tell them we gave all ours to the bank. If they pester you about the old money, you just tell 'em we haven't got money like that in this house.'

'Nan,' I half-laughed, 'no one from the government is gunna come round and do that!'

'Ooh, don't you believe it. You don't know what the government's like, you're too young. You'll find out one day what they can do to people. You never trust anybody who works for the government. You mark my words, Sally.'

I was often puzzled by the way Mum and Nan approached anyone in authority, as if they were frightened. Why on earth would anyone be frightened of the government?

Apart from art and English, I failed nearly everything else in the second term of my third year in high school. Mum was disgusted with my seven per cent for geometry and trigonometry.

'You've got your Junior soon. How on earth do you expect to pass that?'

'I don't care whether I pass or not. Why don't you let me leave school?'

'You'll leave school over my dead body!'

'What's the point in all this education if I'm going to spend the rest of my life drawing and painting?'

'You are not going to spend the rest of your life doing that, there's no future in it. Artists only make money after they're dead and gone.'

I gave up arguing and retreated to my room. Mum never took my ambition to be an artist seriously. Not that she didn't encourage me to draw. Once, when I was bored, she let me paint pictures all over the asbestos sheets that covered in our back verandah. Nan had thought it was real good.

I sighed. Nan believed in my drawings.

The following weekend, my Aunty Judy came to lunch. She was a friend of Mum's. Her family, the Drake-Brock-mans, and ours had known each other for years. 'Sally, I want to have a talk with you about your future,' she said quietly, after we'd finished dessert.

I glared at Mum.

'You know you can't be an artist. They don't get anywhere in this world. You shouldn't worry your mother like that. She wants you to stay at school and finish your Leaving. You can give up all idea of Art School because it's just not on.'

I was absolutely furious. Not because of anything Aunty Judy had said, but because Mum had the nerve to get someone from outside the family to speak to me. Mum walked around looking guilty for the rest of the afternoon.

It wasn't only Mum and Aunty Judy, it was my art teacher at school as well. He held up one of my drawings in front of the class and pointed out everything wrong with it. There was no perspective, I was the only one with no horizon line. My people were flat and floating. You had to turn it on the side to see what half the picture was about. On and on he went. By the end of ten minutes the whole class was laughing and I felt very small. I'd always believed that drawing was my only talent; now I knew I was no good at that, either.

The thought of that horrible day made me want to cry. I was glad I was in my room on my own, because I suddenly felt tears rushing to my eyes and spilling down my cheeks. I decided then to give up drawing. I was sick of banging my head against a brick wall. I got together my collection of drawings and paintings, sneaked down to the back of the yard, and burnt them.

When Mum and Nan found out what I'd done they were horrified.

'All those beautiful pictures,' Nan moaned, 'gone for ever.' Mum just glared at me. I knew she felt she couldn't say too much; after all, she was partly responsible for driving me to it.

It took about a month for Mum and I to make up. She insisted that if I did my Junior, she wouldn't necessarily make me go on to my Leaving. Like a fool, I believed her.

Towards the end of the school year, I arrived home early one day to find Nan sitting at the kitchen table, crying. I froze in the doorway, I'd never seen her cry before.

'Nan...what's wrong?'

'Nothin'!'

'Then what are you crying for?'

She lifted up one arm and thumped her clenched fist hard on the kitchen table. 'You bloody kids don't want me, you want a bloody white grandmother. I'm black. Do you hear, *black, black, black!*' With that she pushed back her chair and hurried out to her room. I continued to stand in the doorway. I could feel the strap of my heavy school-bag cutting into my shoulder, but I was too stunned to remove it.

For the first time in my fifteen years, I was conscious of Nan's colouring. It was true, she wasn't white. Well, I thought logically, if she wasn't white, then neither were we. What did that make us, what did that make me? I had never thought of myself as being black before.

That night, as Jill and I were lying quietly on our beds, looking at a poster of John, Paul, George and Ringo, I said: 'Jill...did you know Nan was black?'

'Course I did.'

'I didn't, I just found out.'

'I know you didn't. You're really dumb, sometimes. You reckon I'm gullible, but some things you just don't see. You know we're not Indian, don't you?'

'Mum said we're Indian.'

'Does Nan look Indian?'

'I've never really thought about how she looks. Maybe she comes from some Indian tribe we don't know about.'

'Ha! That'll be the day! You know what we are, don't you?'

'No, what?'

'Boongs, we're *Boongs!*' I could tell Jill was unhappy

with the idea.

It took a few minutes before I summoned up enough courage to say, 'What's a Boong?'

'You know, Aboriginal. God, of all things, we're Aboriginal!'

'Oh.' I suddenly understood. There was a great deal of social stigma attached to being Aboriginal at our school.

'I can't believe you've never heard the word Boong,' Jill muttered in disgust. 'Haven't you ever listened to the kids at school? If they want to run you down, they say, "Aah, ya just a Boong." Honestly, Sally, you live the whole of your life in a daze!'

Jill was right, I did live in a world of my own. She was much more attuned to our social environment. It was important for her to be accepted at school, because she enjoyed being there.

'You know, Jill,' I said after a while, 'if we are Boongs, and I don't know if we are or not, but *if* we are, there's nothing we can do about it, so we might as well just accept it.'

'Accept it? Can you tell me one good thing about being an Abo?'

'Well, I don't know much about them,' I answered. 'They like animals, don't they? We like animals.'

'A lot of people like animals, Sally. Haven't you heard of the RSPCA?'

'Of course I have! But don't Abos feel close to the earth and all that stuff?'

'I don't know. All I know is none of my friends like them. I've been trying to convince Lee for two years that we're Indian.' Lee was Jill's best friend and her opinions were very important. Lee loved Nan, so I didn't see that it mattered.

'You know Susan?' Jill said, interrupting my thoughts. 'Her mother said she doesn't want her mixing with you because you're a bad influence. She reckons all Abos are a bad influence.'

'Aaah, I don't care about Susan, never liked her much anyway.'

'You still don't understand, do you?' Jill groaned in

disbelief. 'It's a terrible thing to be Aboriginal. Nobody wants to know you, not just Susan. You can be Indian, Dutch, Italian, *anything*, but not Aboriginal! I suppose it's all right for someone like you, you don't care what people think. You don't need anyone, but I do!' Jill pulled her rugs over her head and pretended she'd gone to sleep. I think she was crying, but I had too much new information to think about to try and comfort her. Besides, what could I say?

Nan's outburst over her colouring and Jill's assertion that we were Aboriginal heralded a new phase in my relationship with my mother. I began to pester her incessantly about our background. Mum consistently denied Jill's assertion. She even told me that Nan had come out on a boat from India in the early days. She was so convincing I began to wonder if Jill was right after all.

When I wasn't pestering Mum, I was busy pestering Nan. To my surprise, I discovered Nan had a real short fuse when it came to talking about the past. Whenever I attempted to question her, she either lost her temper or locked herself in her room and wouldn't emerge until it was time for Mum to come home from work. It was a conspiracy.

One night, Mum came into my room and sat on the end of my bed. She had her This Is Serious look on her face. With an unusual amount of firmness in her voice, she said quietly, 'Sally, I want to talk to you.'

I lowered my *Archie* comic. 'What is it?'

'I think you know, don't act dumb with me. You're not to bother Nan any more. She's not as young as she used to be and your questions are making her sick. She never knows when you're going to try to trick her. There's no point in digging up the past; some things are better left buried. Do you understand what I'm saying? You're to leave her alone.'

'Okay, Mum,' I replied glibly, 'but on one condition.'

'What's that?'

'You answer one question for me?'

'What is it?' Poor Mum, she was a trusting soul.

'Are we Aboriginal?'

Mum snorted in anger and stormed out. Jill chuckled

from her bed. 'I don't know why you keep it up. I think it's better not to know for sure, that way you don't have to face up to it.'

'I keep pestering them because I want to know the truth, and I want to hear it from Mum's own lips.'

'It's a lost cause, they'll never tell you.'

'I'll crack 'em one day.'

Jill shrugged good-naturedly and went back to reading her *True Romance* magazine.

I settled back into my mattress and began to think about the past. Were we Aboriginal? I sighed and closed my eyes. A mental picture flashed vividly before me. I was a little girl again, and Nan and I were squatting in the sand near the back steps.

'This is a track, Sally. See how they go.' I watched, entranced, as she made the pattern of a kangaroo. 'Now, this is a goanna and here are emu tracks. You see, they are all different. You got to know all of them if you want to catch tucker.'

'That's real good, Nan.'

'You want me to draw you a picture, Sal?' she said as she picked up a stick.

'Okay.'

'These are men, you see, three men. They are very quiet, they're hunting. Here are kangaroos, they're listening, waiting. They'll take off if they know you're coming.' Nan wiped the sand picture out with her hand. 'It's your turn now,' she said, 'you draw something.'

I grasped the stick eagerly. 'This is Jill and this is me. We're going down the swamp.' I drew some trees and bushes...

I opened my eyes and the picture vanished. Had I remembered something important? I didn't know. That was the trouble. I knew nothing about Aboriginal people. I was clutching at straws.

It wasn't long before I was too caught up in preparations for my Junior examinations to bother too much about where we'd come from. At that time, the Junior was the first major exam in high school. To a large extent it determined your future. If you failed, you automatically left school and looked for a job. If you passed, it was generally accepted that you would do another two years' study and aim for university entrance.

Mum was keen on me doing well, so I decided that, for her, I'd make the effort and try to pass subjects I'd previously failed. For the first time in my school life I actually sat up late, studying my textbooks. It was hard work, but Mum encouraged me by bringing in cups of tea with cake or toast and jam.

After each examination, she'd ask me anxiously how I'd gone. My reply was always, 'Okay.' I never really knew. Sometimes I thought I'd done all right, but then I reasoned that all I needed was a hard marker and I might fail. I didn't want to get Mum's hopes up.

Much to the surprise of the whole family, I passed every subject, even scoring close to the distinction mark in English and art. Mum was elated.

'I knew you could do it! Mr Buddee was right about you.'

Good old Mr Buddee. I didn't know whether to curse or thank him. Now that I had passed my Junior, I sensed there was no hope of Mum allowing me to leave school. I should have deliberately failed, I thought. Then, she wouldn't have had any choice. Actually, I had considered just that, but for some reason I couldn't bring myself to do it. I guess it was my pride again.

14

WHAT PEOPLE ARE WE?

Fourth year high school was supposed to be a transitory year where we were treated more like adults and less like difficult teenagers. Even our classes were supposed to be structured to mimic the kind of organisation we might find later in tertiary institutions. I was a year older, but I was still the same person with the same problems. I felt this was also true of school. The changes were only superficial. However, some deep and important things did happen to me that year.

One day, I happened to bump into a girl I'd been friendly with in my Sunday School days. She invited me to a youth meeting at a nearby church hall.

'Aw, no thanks, Sharon.'

'Look, it's not going to be anything like you might imagine,' she said confidently. 'Nothing to do with religion, just some Chinese food and a bit of a get-together, that's all.'

'You sure?'

'Positive.'

'Okay, I'll come. I know some other kids who like Chinese food. I might bring them, too.'

'Great. See you there.'

I arrived at the meeting with seven girls from around our

neighbourhood and two from school. The food was quite good, and, even though everyone else there ignored us, we enjoyed ourselves. When everyone had finished stuffing themselves, a chap stood up and said, 'We have Mr McLean here to give us a little talk. I'd like you all to be quiet while we listen to what he has to say.'

Uh-oh, I thought. Here it comes. I looked towards the back of the hall. The door was closed and there were two elderly gentlemen standing in front of it. I was trapped. I knew if Mr McLean turned out to be half as boring as some of the teachers I'd had in Sunday School, my friends would never forgive me.

Mr McLean stood up and smiled at us. 'I'm here to talk to you young people about your future,' he said. 'Your eternal future,' I mouthed quietly in unison with Mr McLean. I'd heard it all before.

As he continued, I began to think of other things…the new clothes Mum had promised to buy me, the latest quiz show on TV, the way Jill seemed to be able to whip up an outfit on our old treadle machine in no time at all.

Suddenly, there was someone talking to me. I knew it wasn't Mr McLean. I looked around furtively. All eyes were fixed on the speaker; there was no one new in the room.

'Who are you?' I asked mentally.

With a sudden dreadful insight, I knew it was God.

'What are You doing here?' I asked. I don't know why I was surprised. It was a church hall, after all.

It had to be Him because the voice seemed to come from without, not within; it transcended the reality of the room. I couldn't even see my surroundings any more. I was having an audience with Him, whom I dreaded. The mental pictures I had built up of Him so far in my life began to dissolve, and in their place came a new image. A person, overwhelming love, acceptance and humour. What Nan would call real class. In an instant, I became what others refer to as a believer.

I joined the local youth group after that. I was full of ideas for making our meetings and outings more interesting, but it was difficult to change the pattern set in motion so many years before. I became friendly with Pat, a girl a few years older than me. She was reasonably conservative, but less so than the other girls I'd met, and she had an excellent sense of humour.

One day, she said to me, 'You know, no one here can figure out why you like Youth Group so much, but hate church. What's the difference?'

In Pat's eyes, one was a natural extension of the other. To me, church was practically the antipathy of Youth Group. I always felt uncomfortable in church, it was so formal and lacking in spontaneity. The sermons were full of clichés and things I didn't understand. To me, church was like school, more concerned with red tape than the guts of the matter.

I think Mum was relieved I was finally channelling my energies into what she saw as something creative. Up to now, she hadn't been sure how I'd turn out. She hoped that with the encouragement of people at church, I would begin to lead a more productive and less rebellious life. She was wrong.

One night, one of the deacons asked if he could talk to me. I was friendly with his daughter and he seemed like a nice man.

'You and Mary are having quite a lot to do with one another, aren't you?' he said. 'You see a lot of each other at Youth Group and church.'

'Yeah.'

'Well, Sally, I want to ask a favour of you.' He smiled.

'Sure, anything.'

'I'd like you to stop mixing with Mary.' He gave another charming smile.

'Why?' I was genuinely puzzled.

'I think you know why.'

'No, I don't.'

'You're a bad influence, you must realise that.'

'What do you mean?' I wanted him to spell it out.

'This is Mary's Leaving year, the same as yours. I don't want her mixing with you in case she picks up any of your bad habits.'

Aaah, I thought. He's heard about my truancy.

'What about after Leaving?' I asked meekly. I sensed there was more to this than just that.

'Really, I think it'd be better if you broke off your friendship entirely. You do understand, don't you?'

'Oh, I understand,' I replied. I was amazed that he could have such a charming manner and yet be such a dag.

'Good girl, I knew you would.' He was relieved. 'Oh, by the way. I can count on you not to say anything to Mary, can't I? You'll find a way of breaking things off between you, won't you?'

I nodded my head, and he walked off.

I was hurt and disappointed. He was a deacon, I'd looked up to him. I was lucky I had my pride, it came to my rescue yet again. I didn't need people like him, I decided.

It was about that time that I began to analyse my own attitudes and feelings more closely. I looked at Mum and Nan and I realised that part of my inability to deal constructively with people in authority had come from them. They were completely baffled by the workings of government or its bureaucracies. Whenever there were difficulties, rather than tackle the system directly they'd taught us it was much more effective to circumvent or forestall it. If that didn't work, you could always ignore it.

That summer, the State Housing department decided to paint the exteriors of the houses in our street. A decision that really panicked Nan. She made sure the front and back doors were kept locked so they couldn't come inside, and spent most of the day peeping out at them from behind the curtains.

I tried to reason with her. The fact that State Housing employees had only ever called to collect the rent or carry out routine maintenance meant nothing to Nan. For her, they were here to check on us; the possibility of eviction was always there, hanging over our heads like some invisible guillotine.

I thought back to all the years she had spent buttering up the rentmen. Why did she do it? Why was she afraid? I decided I'd try to talk to her again. Try to explain how things worked.

After she had given the painters a slap-up morning tea, I cornered her out the back, where she was raking up leaves. 'Nan,' I said in a reasonable tone of voice, 'I don't think you understand about the house we rent.'

'What do you mean?' she muttered. She kept her head down and continued to rake.

'Well, you only get evicted if you don't look after the place. For example, if we were to smash a wall or break all the windows they might think about throwing us all out; otherwise, as long as we pay the rent, they'll let us stay.'

'Hmmph, you think you know everything, don't you?' she replied bitterly. 'You don't know nothin', girl. You don't know what it's like for people like us. We got to look out for ourselves.'

'What do you mean, people like us? We're just like anybody else, aren't we?'

'In this world, there's no justice, people like us'd all be dead and gone now if it was up to this country.' She stopped and wiped her mouth with a handkerchief. Her eyes looked tired and wet.

'Nan,' I said carefully, 'what people are we?'

She was immediately on the defensive. She looked sharply at me. 'You're tryin' to trick me again. Aaah, you can't be trusted. I'm not stupid, you know. I'm not saying nothing. Nothing, do you hear?'

I suddenly felt terribly sad. The barriers were up again. Just when I thought I was finally getting somewhere. 'Nan,' I coaxed, 'I'm not trying to trick you. I just want to know what people we are, that's all.'

'I'm not talking,' she muttered as she dropped her rake and put her hands over her ears.

I sighed and walked back to the house. Inside, I felt all churned up, but I didn't know why. I had accepted by now that Nan was dark, that our heritage was not that shared by most Australians, but I hadn't accepted that we were Aboriginal. I was too ignorant to make such a decision, and too confused. I found myself coming back to the same old question: if Nan was Aboriginal, why didn't she just say so? The fact that both Mum and Nan made consistent denials made me think I was barking up the wrong tree. I could see no reason why they would pretend to be something they weren't.

15

MAKE SOMETHING OF YOURSELF

Mum was proving to be quite a successful business woman. She had been doing so well for many years working as a florist that in 1967, with the help of a loan from her old friend Lois, she was able to buy her own business. Things were now really looking up financially.

But she would have been more contented if she could have seen greater evidence that some of her own drive and ambition was rubbing off on her children.

'You want to make something of yourself,' Mum said to me one night. She was going on about wanting me to do well in my Leaving.

I was fed up with hearing that phrase. Mum and Nan were always harping on about how us kids must make something of ourselves.

'I've got no ambitions,' I replied hopelessly. 'I can't see myself doing anything.'

'You've got plenty of talents, you just haven't discovered them yet.'

'Mum, there are more important things than what talents

you've got. I feel pressured by everything else.'

'There's no need for dramatics. What's there for you to worry about?'

How could I tell her it was me, and her and Nan. The sum total of all the things I didn't understand about them or myself. The feeling that a very vital part of me was missing and that I'd never belong anywhere. Never resolve anything.

I suppose it wasn't surprising that I returned to my final year in high school with a rather depressed attitude. One lunch-time, I was talking about families with a girl in my class. When I mentioned mine and said how ordinary they were, she burst out laughing.

'You really think your family's normal?'

'Course they're normal.'

'You've got the most abnormal family I've ever come across! Don't get me wrong, I like your mother, I really do, but the way you all look at life is weird.'

My class-mate continued to chuckle on and off for the rest of the lunch hour. I never asked her to explain further, I was too embarrassed.

Not long after that, I was away from school with a genuine illness, a bout of summer flu. As I lay sprawled on my bed, reading one of Jill's *True Romance* magazines, I gradually became aware of a conversation Nan was having with the rentman on the front porch.

'Just look at that beautiful sky and those fluffy white clouds over there,' she said. 'Isn't it wonderful, what God has made?'

I smiled at her tone of voice, the one she used when she wanted to impress religious people. Nan was a shrewd judge of character. It took only a few minutes for her to sum up a person and then direct her conversation and behaviour accordingly.

'Yes, Nanna, it's wonderful.'

'And look at that black crow over there and all those maggies,' Nan went on eagerly. 'God made them, too.'

Following her lead, the rentman added, 'Yes, and the grass and trees.'

'That's right,' Nan continued, 'and here are you and I, both white, and we couldn't do that!'

My initial reaction to Nan's comment was one of silent, uncontrolled laughter, but within minutes my feelings of amusement had see-sawed down to deep sadness. Why did she want to be white? Did she really equate being white with the power of God? With sudden insight I realised there must have been times in her life when she'd looked around and the evidence was right before her eyes. If you were white, you could do anything.

When it came to economy, I did realise that Mum and Nan had some rather peculiar ideas. I used to wear shoes with the toes stuffed with newspaper 'to grow into'. When I was little, Nan had had to make do with the same clothes year in and year out and there were times when they had both gone without their own tea just to feed us, so I suppose I shouldn't have been surprised by the intensity with which they hoarded everything under the sun. What amazed me was that as our financial situation improved, so their tendency to hoard gained momentum. Before very long, they were both avid collectaholics.

Mum and Nan had always argued, but when it came to disputes over their different stockpiles, the comments became quite pointed. Nan referred to Mum's as broken-down junk, while Mum considered Nan's as good for nothing. Fortunately, there was something they did both agree about: the value of tools.

When Dad was alive, he'd hoarded tools; after he died, Mum and Nan continued to hoard tools, even though there was little use for them. Nan loved tools. They gave her status, and Mum regularly contributed weird and wonderful implements to Nan's growing collection. One afternoon, she returned home from an auction with a large scythe. Nan was really excited and said it was better than a lawnmower.

'That's a stupid thing to buy her,' I berated Mum. 'You know her eyesight's not too good. She might chop a leg off.'

Mum dismissed my fears with a wave of her hand, maintaining that as Nan had used one when she was younger, it was perfectly safe. My curiosity was aroused. I tried to picture Nan as a young girl, swinging a scythe. Where would she have used one, and why? I trooped out to the backyard, where she was busily scything some long grass.

'Hear you used one of those things when you were younger,' I said casually.

'Oh yes,' she replied as she swung away. 'Good for weeds and grass. Kept the garden neat.'

'Whose garden?'

'You never stop, do you. You come sneakin' up, tryin' to trick me. You never been interested in gardens before, Sally!' She turned and continued to hack away. Our conversation was at an end.

At the end of first term, our physics teacher gave the class a little talk.

'It's interesting,' he said, 'only two more terms to go and I can already tell which of you will pass or fail. And I'm not just talking about physics. In this class, most of you will pass. Then there are a few who are borderline, and one who will definitely fail.' He looked at me. 'I don't know why you bother to turn up at all. You might as well throw in the towel now.'

Everyone laughed. I was really mad. Until then, I hadn't cared whether I passed or failed. *I'll prove you wrong, you crumb*, I thought.

During second term, I made sporadic attempts at study. Once the August holidays were over, I began in earnest. I knew it wasn't going to be an easy task. I lacked the photographic memories of my two sisters, and I was way behind in my work. As usual, Mum tried to encourage me by providing every snack imaginable.

Instead of having a good night's sleep before each exam, I kept myself awake by drinking strong coffee and tried to cram as much extra information into my brain as possible. By the end of my exams, I knew I'd passed English, history and economics. I was doubtful about chemistry and I was almost certain I had failed physics, maths 1 and maths 2. I confided none of my fears to Mum. I figured she'd be disappointed soon enough. I needed five subjects to score my Leaving Certificate and I was confident of only three. It seemed all my hard work had been for nothing.

Mum gave me what she considered good advice for every teenager. 'Now that you've finished your exams, you want to go out and let your hair down a bit.' I knew she thought it wasn't normal for a girl my age to be spending so many nights at home.

'Look, Mum, will you give it a rest?' I yelled. I'd had a short fuse since my exams. 'I just want to sit here and be left in peace!'

Poor Mum, she now had within her family two extremes. On the one hand, there was me attending prayer meetings, and on the other, there were Jill and Bill. Like normal teenagers, they spent their weekends raging about Perth. Bill had just completed his Junior Certificate exams.

I was becoming very worried about my Leaving results. They were printed every year in the *West Australian* and I thought this was terrible because it meant your shame was made public. Sometimes, other people knew even before you whether you'd failed or not. I could cope with the public exposure, but what about Mum? She'd always boasted to the neighbours about how bright all her children were. It would be a real slap in the face if they should see her eldest daughter's name in print with a string of fails after it. There was only one thing to do: disappear. I volunteered to help out at some church camps for young children. I would be away when the results came out.

Camp proved an interesting experience for me. I'd always enjoyed the company of small children. I had a group of ten to look after, and two of the girls were Aboriginal. They talked to me about their lives at home and which part of the country their Mums and Dads had come from. I seemed to have a natural affinity with them. That wasn't to say that I didn't get on well with the others, but I felt I had a special insight into the Aboriginal girls.

A few days before the results were due to come out, Mum rang to see how I was and to ask which bus I was coming home on.

'I'm not coming,' I told her firmly. 'They're short of helpers here so I'm staying on.'

'Don't you want to read your results in the paper?'

'I'm in Rockingham, Mum, not Africa, they get the paper down here too.'

'Sally,' she said suspiciously, 'you're not staying away because you think you've failed?'

'We-ell...'

'Oh, what's to become of you?' Mum wailed.

'Don't go weepy on me, Mum,' I implored. 'I might have passed.'

We both hung up at the same time.

The day the results came out, I received a long, mushy telegram from Mum, extolling my superior intelligence and patting me on the back for passing five subjects. By the time I returned from camp, she had convinced herself that I'd go to university and become a doctor.

She was very disappointed in my decision never to study again. I told her I was sick of people telling me what to do with my life. I wanted to work, to earn some money. I wanted to be independent.

'But Sally,' she protested, 'you're the first one in our family to have gone this far. Why can't you go to university? What about becoming a vet? When you were little, you loved looking after sick animals.' I opened my mouth to protest, but Mum cut me off. 'I know you were always worried about having to treat a sick snake, but I'm sure that'd be rare and you could always sedate them.'

'Mum,' I groaned, 'I just don't want to do any more study.'

'So you've come all this way for nothing? You're too stubborn for your own good. You'll regret it one day, you mark my words.'

'Oh, stop complaining. You're lucky I lasted this long. Aren't you pleased you'll be having a bit of extra money coming in?'

'I never worried about the money. All that work,' Mum bemoaned.

Shortly after that, I began attending Saturday afternoon basketball matches. Not to play, just to watch. By then, as a result of camp, I'd made some good friends with girls from other churches. When their games were finished, we'd stroll down to watch the boys' basketball.

I'd been hearing about a girl who attended a church a few suburbs from mine who was supposed to have a great personality and sense of humour. I was keen to meet her. Firstly, because I hadn't met many girls with a great sense of humour, and secondly, because I'd come in on quite a few conversations about this girl that had ended with, 'Yeah, but she's got a great personality,' or, 'Yeah, but she's nice, isn't she?' I wondered what was wrong with her.

When we finally met, I understood. I can't remember her name, but she was a very dark Aboriginal girl. We became friends and I enjoyed her company on Saturday afternoons.

One day, she told me she was leaving.

'Where are you going?' I asked.

'I'm going back to live with my people.'

'Your people?' I was so dumb.

'Yes. I'm going back to live with them. I want to help them if I can.'

I was really sorry I wouldn't be seeing her any more. And I wondered who her people were and why they needed help. What was wrong with them? I was too embarrassed to ask.

In 1969 I managed to secure a job as a clerk in a government department. It was incredibly boring — I had nothing to do. I begged my superiors to give me more work, but they said there was none. Like them, I just had to master the art of looking busy. A couple of weeks, I was even forced to work overtime: not that there was anything to do, but they were all working overtime and they said it would look bad if I didn't, too. In desperation, I took to hiding novels in government files; that way, I could sit at my desk and read without everyone telling me, 'Look busy, girl. Look busy!'

I lasted there about six months, then I resigned. And I thought school was boring! That was my first experience of being employed and I hadn't liked it one bit. It was an important experience for me, because it taught me something about myself that I had been unaware of. I wasn't going to be satisfied with just anything. And I wasn't lazy.

I had been unemployed about four months when I decided that it was time I began looking for other work. I was sick of sitting around at home with little to do.

I found a job as a laboratory assistant. For some reason, my new employer assumed that as I had studied physics and chemistry at school, I must know something about them. My job was to analyse mineral samples from different parts of Western Australia for tin, iron oxide, and so on.

I accidentally disposed of my first lot of samples, so in desperation I invented the results. My boss was quite excited. 'Hmmm,' he said, as he looked over my recording sheet, 'these aren't bad. Good girl!'

I felt so guilty; I imagined that on the basis of my analysis, they might begin drilling straight away in the hope of a big strike. I took more care after that.

The women I worked with all had strong personalities. Our boss was hardly ever in so we took extended lunch hours and had long conversations about whatever came into our heads. I was very impressed with the whole group. They were the first females I'd met who actually had something to say. One of them confided to me that she was schizophrenic. It was a confidence that failed to enlighten me; I just wondered what country she came from.

One day, I returned to the office from my lunch hour to find everyone abnormally subdued. Our office was going to be moved away from the city. It meant that the whole company, instead of maintaining small branches here and there, would be under one roof. We would all have to knuckle under and behave. I decided to resign. My boss offered me a rise in pay if I stayed. He said I was the best laboratory assistant they'd ever had. Then the decision was taken out of my hands when I suddenly developed industrial acne as a result of being allergic to the chemicals I was using.

By the time I left the laboratory job, I had developed an interest in psychology. I had looked up 'schizophrenic' in my dictionary and found out it was not a nationality after all.

I was more realistic about myself now. I realised that the chances of finding a job I would really enjoy were remote. I needed to do further study. I decided to enrol in university for the following year, along with Jill. Having now completed her Leaving, she was keen to study Law.

16

UNIVERSITY

Mum was both surprised and pleased when I began university in February. She took it to mean I was, at last, getting somewhere in the world.

I found it to my liking. I was amazed that none of the lecturers checked to see whether you turned up or not. Even missing tutorials wasn't a deadly sin. I spent many long afternoons in the library, reading books totally unrelated to my course. Then there were hours in the coffee shop, discussing the meaning of life, and days stretched out in the sun under the giant palms that dotted the campus.

Jill was more conscientious than me. It was probably just as well we weren't both doing Arts, because I would have led her astray.

I was studying on a Repatriation scholarship and while there was never any money left over, my needs were small. Apart from my bus fares and lunches, I had few expenses.

I found travelling to university in winter terrible. I hated the cold. I had to catch two buses and they rarely connected in time for me to transfer immediately from one to the other. On really wet, stormy days, I stayed at home. I would sit in front of the fire all day, watch television, and read my latest book from the library. Nan always brought me a huge lunch. It amazed me that after all those years, she was still trying to fatten me up. My brother David and I were her only failures.

The only day she didn't make my lunch was rent day. She was always too busy bustling around preparing the rentman's morning tea. One morning, she was being particularly fussy. It was a new rentman's first visit and Nan wanted to impress him. She sat on the front porch with him, and when she returned inside, the large plate of biscuits she'd laid out was completely empty.

'Goodness me, he must have liked that lot,' I said.

Nan smiled. 'He loved them. That poor man was so hungry he ate the lot! He asked me what brand they were, but I didn't know.' Nan shoved a paper and pencil into my hands. 'Write down the name for me. The empty packet's over there on the bench.'

'What? This one?' I leant weakly against the side of the bench.

'What are you laughing for?'

With an unsteady hand, I held the empty packet as close as I could to her face. Her mouth dropped open in shock as her gaze took in the half-torn picture of a fox terrier.

'No supper for Curly tonight, Nan,' I choked. Curly was our latest dog.

Over the next few months, the fact that Nan's eyesight was failing became obvious. Sometimes, she mistook the salt for the sugar or the deodorant for the flyspray. We complained, but Mum was prepared to tolerate all these little mistakes — until, one evening, Nan made a fatal error.

It was Friday night. As usual, Mum had collapsed on the lounge in front of the TV. She preferred sleeping on the lounge to her own bed, maintaining that television was both relaxing and good company. She was completely covered in several layers of a tartan rug; only her frizzy mop of black curly hair protruded.

It was way past tea-time when Nan entered, carrying a quivering mass of dog food, a brown jellied concoction. I watched curiously as she paused in the doorway and peered intently into the semi-darkness. Her squinting eyes paused for a moment on me. I don't know whether she actually registered my presence, or saw me merely as part of the large green chair I was sitting in. I was about to speak when she turned and, halting abruptly, stared hard at the lounge. She leant forward slightly, her eyes narrowing in concentration, then, moving towards the lounge, she croaked in exasperation, 'There you are, Curly, you stupid dog, didn't you hear me calling you?'

I suppose I should have said something, but my sense of humour got the better of me.

'Come on, Curly,' Nan growled, 'it's no use pretending you're not there.' She moved closer and held out the bowl. 'Eat up now, I'm not standing here all night!' And Nan shoved the food deeper into what she was convinced was Curly's black, furry face.

I watched, entranced, as, prodded into consciousness, the tartan mass that was Mum slowly began to move. Nan, sensing that Curly was at last responding, said, 'Good boy. Good dog. Come and eat it up!'

With one wild fling, Mum emerged. Her frizzy black hair was covered with small chunks of jellied meat.

'Glad?' croaked Nan in disbelief.

'You stupid woman,' Mum spluttered, 'what do you think you're doing?'

It was only after Mum had shampooed her hair and settled back on the lounge with a hot cup of tea that she was able to laugh.

Three sharp barks at the front door then let us know that the recalcitrant Curly was outside and eager to come in. I opened the door and he pattered in, whining, a sure sign that he was hungry. Nan poked her head around the kitchen doorway and whispered, 'Is that Curly, Sally?'

'I think so,' I laughed, 'unless Mum barks too.'

Nan chuckled, then said, 'Come on, Curly, you naughty boy. Where have you been? Glad nearly got your tea!'

The following week, Mum bought Nan a pair of old

binoculars. Nan was really excited. All of a sudden, she could see things that had been blurred for years.

By the time I'd been at university a term, I was finding it very difficult to study at home. Apart from the high noise level and general chaos, I had no desk to work at, and being disorganised, I was always losing important notes and papers.

When the August holidays came around, it suddenly dawned on me that if I was to pass anything, I would actually have to do some work. The trouble was I'd missed out on so much I didn't know where to begin.

My first attempts at a concentrated effort were rather futile. I had to keep interrupting my study to call out, 'Turn down that radio!' or, 'The TV's too loud!' or, 'Will you all shut up, I'm trying to study!'

After a week or so of constant yelling and arguing, I came to the realisation that it was impossible to change my environment. I decided to try to change myself instead. I found that if I tried really hard, I could work amidst the greatest mess and loudest noise level with no bother whatsoever. I just switched off and pretended I was the only one in the house.

This was no mean feat, because our house was always full of people. Many of my brother David's friends would just doss down on the lounge-room floor. They loved staying overnight. David had just begun high school that year. It never occurred to any of us to tell Mum there'd be someone extra for tea. We just assumed that she'd make what she had go a little bit further. I have to admit I was one of the worst offenders, but Mum never complained. She always told us, 'Your friends are welcome in this house.'

My technique for passing my exams that first year was simple, I crammed. The knowledge I gained was of little use to me afterwards, because as soon as my exams were over, I deleted it from my memory. I passed that year with a B and three C's. Mum was pleased, but urged me to spend more time studying so that I could score A's, like Jill.

I decided I would like to spend my second year at university living away from home. Mum was mortified by the idea. I would be the first to leave the family nest. After weeks of tearful arguments, she relented and said that if the Repatriation Department agreed to pay my fees, I could go. Fortunately they did agree, and I was soon ensconced in my own little room at Currie Hall, a co-educational boarding-house opposite the university.

For most of my teenage years, Mum had been concerned over my lack of interest in boys. I had plenty of good friendships with the opposite sex, but never a real romance. She was worried I would end up an old maid, and she herself with no grandchildren. But now that I was living in a co-ed college, she suddenly started worrying that I would join the permissive society. It was difficult for Mum to let me grow up.

I met Paul Morgan through his brother. In fact, Bruce had lived with our family for a while. He was like a brother to me and also a favourite of Nan's. Bruce was a lot like my brother Bill. Paul was a schoolteacher.

Nan never disappeared when Paul or Bruce were around. She actually seemed to enjoy their company. Paul commented once that Nan reminded him of many of the old people who had looked after him up North. I just nodded. It never occurred to me at the time to think about who those people were.

In a short period, Paul and I got to know each other well. We discovered we had a lot in common. I liked the artistic side of his nature and he seemed to find my wit amusing.

Paul had spent his childhood in the north-west, living mostly at Derby. His parents were missionaries, as were his grandparents and many of his relatives. When Paul was thirteen, his family moved to Perth, where his parents started a hostel for mission children who came to the city to attend high school. Paul found high school very difficult at first. Apart from the normal adjustments all children have to make and the fact that he had come from a vastly different environment, he had a language problem. He spoke only pidgin English.

By the end of the second term of my third year at university, we'd fallen in love and decided to get married. This came as a real shock to Mum, because I had always told her Paul was just another good friend. It took a few weeks before the fact that we meant what we said actually sank in. Then Mum reacted more normally: she panicked.

I added to her trauma by telling her I'd decided to be married in our backyard. This immediately prompted her to worry about how she could manage to lock up all the chooks so they didn't molest my wedding guests.

Mum pushed one panic button after another over the following weeks. The drive was too sandy, the grass too prickly and nearly dead, she didn't have enough chairs or glasses or plates. How much food would we need, how many guests would be coming... I told her that there'd be about one hundred people. I thought this would allay her fears, but it only served to heighten them. Then she began asking me whether they were big eaters or small eaters, drinkers or non-drinkers, and so on. In the end, I told her quite sternly: 'Pull yourself together. You're the mother of the bride, you've got to stop worrying and get organised. Think of it as a challenge!'

It was the best advice I could have given her. There was nothing Mum loved more than a challenge.

Our wedding date was set for two months hence. As the days passed, Mum swung into action like a real trooper. Every morning and night she watered the grass in an attempt to coax back the green colour normally associated with lawn. For some reason, the drive became the focal point of all her worries. One afternoon, a huge load of gravel was deposited on our verge. Three days later, a cement roller weighing about a ton arrived. In the meantime, Bill had agreed to help rake out the gravel over the drive, but when he saw the cement roller, he looked at Mum in disgust. 'What is that?' he asked.

'It's to help flatten the gravel. You know, make it more

like bitumen.'

Bill scratched his head and breathed out, 'Yeah...and how are we going to get it moving?'

Mum was not to be put off. 'Look, it's got these two sticks poking out, I thought you boys could strap yourselves between them and pull it along.'

'Mother dear,' Bill said between clenched teeth, 'if you think I'm gunna strap myself to that thing, you've got another think coming. Sorry, Sal,' he said as he turned to me, 'not even for you.'

'That's okay, Bill, it was Mum's idea.'

'It wouldn't hurt you.' Mum was offended. 'You know the wedding's soon and I'm worried about the drive.' But Bill was not to be persuaded. He had this knack of recognising the futility of Mum's schemes right from the start.

When Mum approached David the following day, he was more sympathetic. After she pleaded with him, he promised to give it a go. It was nearly a hundred degrees in the shade the day he strapped himself to the roller. Mum cheered him on with glasses of cold lemonade and comments like, 'You're the only one who does anything for me, David.' This kept him going for a couple of hours, but as the temperature continued to rise, his strength sapped.

'I'm not doin' any more, Mum. Bill was right, it's a stupid idea!'

'But you can't leave the drive like that,' Mum protested. 'It's all uneven.'

'You pull it, then!' he shouted. 'Have you any idea how heavy it is? Well, have you?' Weak as he was, he still managed to raise his voice loud enough to cower Mum into silence.

Mum spent the following week working on me. She told me in detail how bad the drive was and hinted that Paul might like to take a turn.

The following Saturday, after lunch, we led him like a lamb to the slaughter. Mum, anxious to get him started, indicated what was expected of him. Paul looked desperately at me. Mum departed down the drive, stomping on the uneven bits in an attempt to press them down.

'Please?' I pleaded.

'All right,' he relented. Removing his shirt, he strapped himself to the roller and began to move after Mum.

'Oh Paul, that's good,' Mum encouraged. 'You're much better than David.'

He laboured admirably for two hours, then staggered inside, dripping with sweat, and collapsed on the lounge.

'Listen, Sal,' he gasped. 'People can break their ankles for all I care. I'm not pulling that roller another inch.'

Just then, Mum entered with more lemonade. 'Drink this, you're a silly boy working in that heat. You're lucky you didn't dehydrate.' Paul choked on the lemonade and then looked at Mum in amazement. 'It wasn't my idea to flatten out the gravel.'

'You've done a wonderful job, Paul. Hasn't he, Jill?'

Jill burst out laughing and fled to the kitchen.

'Is she always like this?' Paul asked me pitifully.

'No,' I replied. 'Normally, she's worse.'

17

OWNING UP

My wedding day, 9 December 1972, dawned bright and sunny. I nicked into town early that morning to buy a wedding dress. I found an Indian caftan that I liked, cream with gold embroidery down the front. It was becoming obvious that the day was going to be a stinker. By the time I got home, the temperature was over forty degrees.

Aunty Vi arrived early to help. She had been a close friend of Mum's in her teenage years and they were both florists.

Mum welcomed her with open arms. Our laundry was jammed with buckets and buckets of cut flowers.

'Mum,' I complained as I tried to fight my way through the buckets to the toilet, 'you won't need all these flowers — and what on earth are these for?' I had spied a huge carton of plastic roses.

Mum poked her head around the laundry door and said crossly, 'Never mind what they're for. You just stay out of the way.'

I was suspicious by then. 'You're not up to anything silly, are you Mum?'

'Of course she isn't,' Nan grumbled as she came to her rescue. 'Now you hurry up and get out of here. We've got work to do.'

'Well, listen Nan,' I said, 'make sure you lock up the chooks, won't you?'

'Oh, the chooks are all right,' she replied. 'They're having their scratch around now. I'll pen them up before anyone comes.'

Just then, Paul's parents arrived. I made the introductions and then, just as I was about to head for the shower, Bill came in. 'Sal,' he said, 'I think we'd better have a talk. There's something I'd like to say to you.'

'Sure Bill, what is it?'

'I just wanted you to know this. If Paul doesn't ever do the right thing by you, you let me know. I'll fix things up.'

'I'll remember that, Bill,' I said. 'But Paul's a nice bloke. I don't think we'll have any problems.'

'Yeah, well, just thought I'd say that to you, okay?'

'Thanks, Bill.' I couldn't help thinking that Mum's prophecy after Dad died had finally come true. Bill really was the man of our house. I felt very lucky. I had a wonderful family.

When I emerged from the shower, I found Mr Morgan busily stacking up glasses in the kitchen. I wandered out the back and to my surprise saw Mum, Aunty Vi and Mrs Morgan squatting on their knees in the dirt. They were surrounded by buckets and buckets of cut flowers. 'That's right, Margaret,' Mum said coaxingly to my future mother-in-law, 'just stick them straight in like that. No one will know the difference.'

'I'll go round and do the front,' said Aunty Vi. She picked up two buckets and shuffled around the side of the house. Just then, Nan joined them. 'I've put all those plastic roses in the front garden, Glad,' she said. 'They look beautiful. You'd think they were real.'

Oh no, I thought. They can't be doing this! I raced back in through the house and out to the front. Garishly coloured flowers of all descriptions were stuck in what had previously been bare earth. They stood straight up, their faces towards the sun.

Mum appeared behind me. 'Oh Sally, what are you doing

here?' she asked nervously.

'MUM! How could you!'

'Well, I told you I was worried about the garden,' she replied lamely.

'It's so embarrassing! How could you ask Margaret Morgan to help? What an introduction to our family! Honestly, Mum, this is one of the stupidest things you've ever done!'

'But the garden looks lovely now. No one will know they're standing there with no roots.'

'It's a stinking hot day. They'll keel over in half an hour.'

'No, they won't. Nan's keeping the sprinkler on them right up till the guests start arriving.'

'Oh, Mum,' I wailed, 'you'll never change!'

By this time, she was looking hot and bothered and extremely harrassed. 'Look,' I said, weakening, 'I'll pretend I didn't see the flowers. But at least make sure the chooks are kept out of the way.'

'Yes, dear.'

Everything seemed to go smoothly after that. The wedding ceremony was brief and to the point. After it was over, I went in search of Nan. I'd been concerned that with the yard full of people she considered strangers, she might pull one of her disappearing acts. Mum had already explained to her that it was important she should be seen as she was the grandmother of the bride. It took me a while to locate her. I finally found her behind our old garden shed, crying.

'Nan, what's wrong?'

'You kids don't need me any more,' she sobbed, 'you're all grown up now.'

'We still need you.' I tried to reassure her. She shook her head and continued to cry.

'Would you like me to get Mum?' I asked anxiously.

She nodded.

I patted her arm and went and explained to Mum about Nan, and she went to comfort her. She persuaded Nan to go inside the house, where she settled her down with a cup of tea.

The rest of the afternoon wasn't too traumatic. Little

things like the chooks and dogs running wild didn't seem to matter. Everyone enjoyed themselves and quite a few people commented that it was the most unusual wedding they'd ever been to. Mum took this as a compliment.

It was close to midnight when the last guest finally left. No one had wanted to go home.

'I did all right, didn't I, Sally?' Mum asked smugly.

'Yeah,' I replied, 'maybe you should go into the catering business.'

'I was thinking that myself!' I glanced at her in astonishment. We both laughed.

Shortly after my wedding, I found out that I had passed all my units at university except psychology. I wasn't surprised. I disliked the second-year work connected with the subject so much that I hadn't bothered to study for my exams. I wanted to change my major for the following year, but Paul talked me out of it. 'You'll have to repeat,' he said.

I was disgusted at the thought. However, I'd heard there was some human content in third-year psychology. So I decided to persevere.

Towards the end of the summer vacation, Paul and I moved into a rundown old weatherboard house in South Perth. The toilet was miles down the back of the yard, only one gas burner worked on the stove, the hot-water system was worse than the old chip heater at home, and the place was infested with tiny sand fleas. After living there a few weeks, we also discovered that there were rats residing underneath the floorboards. For some reason, none of this bothered us. We thought the place had character and it was adventurous being on our own.

After a while, Jill moved in with us, then two other friends as well. We were a happy little group. Most of our evenings were filled with Bob Dylan music, poetry and long discussions about current world issues. It was a lovely time in my life.

The day the university year began, I had to force myself to attend. I was convinced I was going to fail again. Many times

I came near to giving up my course entirely, but Paul always talked me into continuing. He gave me the impression that some of my attitudes were very immature. That was quite a shock. I had never thought of myself as being immature before.

Now that Jill and I were once again living in the same house, we often had long talks about our childhood. And the subject of Nan's origins always came up.

'We'll never know for sure,' Jill said one night. 'Mum will never tell us.'

'I might start pestering her again. We're older now, we've got a right to know.'

'What does Paul think?'

'When I asked him whether he thought Nan was Aboriginal, he just laughed and said, "Isn't it obvious? Of course she is."' Paul, of course, had been brought up with Aboriginal people.

'I don't think we can really decide until we hear Mum admit it from her own lips.'

'That'll be the day.'

A few weeks later, Mum popped in for her usual visit, laden with cakes and eager to tell me about the latest bargain she'd bought at auction. I'd been to many auctions with Mum in the past, and knew that items that looked like bargains at first glance turned out to be a total waste of money on closer inspection. The auctioneers had become so used to Mum buying things no one else wanted that they often knocked things down to her without taking any bids from the floor.

'One-o-four will have it,' they'd shout, as a hammer without a handle or a duplicating machine that didn't duplicate came up for grabs. 'You'll have it, won't you, One-o-four, you buy anything for a dollar.' One-o-four was Mum's permanent bidding number.

'Come out to the car and see what I've bought,' Mum said excitedly. 'You won't believe it.'

As she opened up the back of the car, she said generously,

'You can have whatever you like, there's plenty here.' Mum always bought in bulk.

Apart from the usual assortment of rusty tools and various other odds and ends, Mum had, in fact, actually bought something useful. A box of Indian cheesecloth shirts. There were another seven boxes that had to be picked up later. Approximately 140 shirts in all.

'I'll sell what we can't use at Trash and Treasure,' Mum said. That wasn't a good suggestion — Mum always came home from those markets with more than she had taken.

'Aargh! I don't even want to think about it. Let's go and eat that cake you brought.'

We settled down in the kitchen and I made a cup of tea. Mum was soon in a relaxed and talkative mood. After a while, there was a lull in the conversation, so I said very casually, 'We're Aboriginal, aren't we, Mum?'

'Yes, dear,' she replied, without thinking.

'Do you realise what you just said?' I grinned triumphantly.

Mum put her cake back onto her plate and looked as though she was going to be sick.

'Don't you back down!' I said quickly. 'There've been too many skeletons in our family closet. It's time things came out in the open.'

After a few minutes' strained silence, Mum said, 'Why shouldn't you kids know now? It's not as though you're little any more. Besides, it's different now.'

'All those years, Mum,' I said. 'How could you have lied to us all those years?'

'It was only a little white lie,' she replied sadly.

I couldn't help laughing at her unintentional humour. In no time at all, we were both giggling uncontrollably. It was as if a wall that had been between us suddenly crumbled away. I felt closer to Mum then than I had for years.

18

A BEGINNING

I was very excited by my new heritage. When I told Jill what Mum had said, she replied, 'I don't know what you're making a fuss about. I told you years ago Nan was Aboriginal. The fact that Mum's owned up doesn't change anything.' Sometimes, Jill was so logical I wanted to hit her.

'Jill, it does mean something, to have admitted it. Now she might tell us more about the past. Don't you want to know?'

'Yeah, I guess so, but there's probably not much to tell.'

'There could be tons we don't know. What other skeletons are lurking in the cupboard? I'm going to keep pestering her now till she tells us the whole story.'

'She won't tell you any more.'

'Maybe not,' I replied, 'but the way I look at it, it's a beginning. Before, we had nothing.'

When Mum popped in a week later with a large sponge cake filled with chocolate custard, I was ecstatic. Not because of the cake, but because I had a bombshell to drop, and I was anxious to get on with it. I made coffee for a change and waited until Mum was halfway through a piece of sponge before I said, 'I've applied for an Aboriginal scholarship.'

'What!' She choked as she slammed down her mug.

'There's an Aboriginal scholarship you can get, Mum. Anyone of Aboriginal descent is eligible to apply.'

'Oh Sally, you can't.'

'Why can't I,' I demanded, 'or are you going to tell me that Nan's really Indian after all?'

'Oh Sally, you're awful.' Mum chuckled, then added thoughtfully, 'Well, why shouldn't you apply? Nan's had a hard life. Why shouldn't her grandchildren get something out of it?'

I don't think Mum realised how deep my feelings went. It wasn't the money I was after, I was still receiving the Repatriation scholarship. I desperately wanted to do something to identify with my new-found heritage.

When I was granted an interview for my scholarship application, Mum was very worried about what I was going to tell them. Mum always worried about what to tell people. It was as if the truth was never adequate, or else there was something to hide. She had been inventing stories and making exaggerated claims since the day she was born. It was part of her personality. She found it difficult to imagine how anyone could get through life any other way. Consequently, when I answered, in response to her question about my interview, 'I'm going to tell them the truth,' she was flabbergasted.

I was successful in my scholarship application, but for the next few months, I was the butt of many family jokes. We all felt shy and awkward about our new-found past. No one was sure whether I'd done the right thing or not. In keeping with my character, I had leapt in feet first. I wanted to do something positive. I wanted to say, 'My grandmother's Aboriginal and it's a part of me, too.' I wasn't sure where my actions would lead and the fact that Nan remained singularly unimpressed with my efforts only added confusion to my already tenuous sense of identity.

'Did Mum tell you I got the scholarship, Nan?' I asked one day.

'Yes. What did you tell them?'

'I told them that our family was Aboriginal but that we'd been brought up to believe differently.'

'What did you tell them about me?'

'Nothing.'

'You won't ever tell them about me, will you, Sally? I don't like strangers knowing our business, especially government people. You never know what they might do.'

'Why are you so suspicious, Nan?' I asked gently. She ignored my question and shuffled outside to the garden. A sense of sadness suddenly overwhelmed me. I wanted to cry. 'Get a grip on yourself,' I muttered. 'You don't even know what you want to cry about!'

Slowly, over that year, Mum and I began to notice a change in Nan. Her interests began to extend beyond who was in the telephone box opposite our house to world affairs. Nan had always watched the news every night on each channel if she could, but now, instead of just noting world disasters, she began to take an interest in news about black people. If the story was sad, she'd put her hand to her mouth and say, 'See, see what they do to black people.' On the other hand, if black people were doing well for themselves, she'd complain, 'Just look at them, showing off. Who do they think they are? They just black like me.'

About this time, Nan's favourite word became 'Nyoongah'*. She'd heard it used on a television report and had taken an instant liking to it. To Nan, anyone dark was now Nyoongah. Africans, Burmese, American Negroes were all Nyoongahs. She identified with them. In a sense, they were her people, because they shared the common bond of blackness and the oppression that, for so long, that colour had brought. It was only a small change, but it was a beginning.

In a strange sort of way, my life had new purpose because of that. I wondered whether, because Jill and I had accepted

* *Nyoongah* — the Aboriginal people of south-west Australia. (Derived from 'man' or 'person'. Also the language of these people.)

the Aboriginal part of ourselves, perhaps Nan was coming to terms with it, too. I was anxious to learn as much as I could about the past.

'Where was Nan born?' I asked Mum one day.

'Oh, I don't know. Up North somewhere.'

'Has she ever talked to you about her life?'

'You know she won't talk about the past. She says she can't remember.'

'Do you think she does remember?'

'I think so, but she thinks we're prying, trying to hurt her.'

'Mum, is there anyone who could tell me anything about Nan?'

'Only Judy.'

'Aunty Judy?'

'Yes. Nan worked for their family.'

'In what capacity?'

'Oh, you know, housework, that sort of thing.'

'You mean she was a servant?'

'Yes, I suppose so.' ·

'How long did she work for them?'

'Oh, I don't know, Sally. Why do you always bring this up? Can't we talk about something else?' Nearly all our conversations ended like that.

Amazingly, I passed my psychology unit at the end of that year; I even scored a B. I was looking forward to my final year because there was quite a large slice about people in the course and that, after all, was what I'd come to learn about.

By now, both Jill and I had many friends at university. All our lives, people had asked us what nationality we were. Most assumed we were Greek or Italian, but we'd always replied, 'Indian.' Now, when we were asked, we said, 'Aboriginal.'

We often swapped tales of what the latest comment was. A few of our acquaintances said, 'Aaah, you're only on the scholarship because of the money.' At that time, the Aboriginal allowance exceeded the allowance most students got. We felt embarrassed when anyone said that, because we knew it must seem like that. We had suddenly switched our allegiance from India to Aboriginal Australia and they could see no reason why we would do that except for the money.

Sometimes, people would say, 'You're lucky, you'd never know you were that, you could pass for anything.' Others reacted with an embarrassed silence. Perhaps that was the worst reaction of all. It was as though we'd said a forbidden word. Others muttered, 'Oh, I'm sorry...' and when they realised what they were saying, they just sort of faded away.

Until now, if we thought about it at all, we'd both considered Australia the least racist country in the world. Now we knew better. I began to wonder what it was like for Aboriginal people with really dark skin and broad features. How did Australians react to them? How had white Australians reacted to my grandmother in the past? Was that the cause of her bitterness?

About halfway through 1973, I received a brief note from the Commonwealth Department of Education, asking me to an interview with a senior officer of the department.

Two days later, I sat nervously in the waiting area. I had pains in my stomach. I always got pains in my stomach when I was nervous. Several people walked past and eyed me curiously. I suddenly had the distinct impression that something was wrong.

'You may go in now,' the woman at the reception desk said.

'Thanks.' I smiled and walked into the office.

'Mrs Morgan,' the senior officer said as I sat down, 'we'll get straight to the point. We have received information, from what appears to be a reliable source, that you have obtained the Aboriginal scholarship under false pretences. This person, a close friend of you and your sister, has told us that you have been bragging all over the university campus about how easy it is to obtain the scholarship without even being Aboriginal. Apparently, you've been saying that anyone can get it.'

I was so amazed at the ridiculousness of the accusation that I burst out laughing. A tactical error on my part.

'This is no laughing matter. It is a serious offence. Have you lied to this department? I want to hear what you have to say for yourself.'

I felt very angry. It was obvious I had been judged guilty already, and I knew why. It was because Jill and I were doing well. The department never expected any of their Aboriginal students to do well at tertiary studies. They would have considered it more in keeping if we both failed consistently.

'Who made the complaint?'

'I can't tell you. We promised confidentiality.'

'It was no friend of ours.'

'This person is a student and knows you both well.'

'But that doesn't add up. If they know us really well, they would have been to our home and met my grandmother and mother, in which case they'd never have made this complaint.'

'Is that all you have to say?'

'You've obviously already judged me guilty. What else can I say?'

'I expected more than that from you. You don't seem very keen to prove your innocence.'

I'd had it by then. 'Look,' I said angrily, 'when I applied for this scholarship, I told your people everything I knew about my family. It was their decision to grant me a scholarship, so if there's any blame to be laid, it's your fault, not mine. How do you expect me to prove anything? What would you like me to do, bring my grandmother and mother in and parade them up and down so you can all have a look? There's no way I'll do that, even if you tell me to. I'd rather lose the allowance. It's my word against whoever complained, so it's up to you to decide, isn't it?'

My heart was pounding fiercely. It was very difficult for me to stand up for myself; I wasn't used to dealing with authority figures so directly. No wonder Mum and Nan didn't like dealing with government people, I thought. They don't give you a chance.

The senior officer looked at me silently for a few minutes and then said, 'Well, Mrs Morgan. You are either telling the truth, or you're a very good actress!'

I was amazed. Still my innocence wasn't to be conceded.
'I'm telling the truth,' I said.

'Very well, you may go.' I was dismissed with a nod of the head, but I was unable to move.

'I'm not sure I want this scholarship any more,' I said. 'What if someone else makes a complaint? Will I be hauled in here for the same thing?'

The senior officer thought for a moment, then said, 'No. If someone else complains, we'll ignore it.'

Satisfied, I left and walked quickly to the elevator. I felt sick and I wasn't sure how much longer my legs would support me. It was just as well I'd lost my temper, I thought. Otherwise, I wouldn't have defended myself at all. It was the thought that somehow Mum and Nan might have to be involved that had angered me. It had seemed so demeaning.

Once outside, I let the breeze blowing up the street ease away my tenseness. I walked slowly to the bus stop. What if I had been too shy to defend myself? What would have happened then? I had no doubt they would have taken the scholarship away from me. Then I thought, maybe I'm doing the wrong thing. It hadn't been easy trying to identify with being Aboriginal. No one was sympathetic. So many people equated it with dollars and cents; no one understood why it was important. I should chuck it all in, I thought. Paul was supporting me now, I could finish my studies without the scholarship. It wasn't worth it.

I wanted to cry. I hated myself when I got like that. I never cried, and yet, since all this had been going on, I'd wanted to cry often. It wasn't something I could control. Sometimes when I looked at Nan, I just wanted to cry. It was absurd. There was so much about myself I didn't understand.

The bus pulled in. I hopped on, paid my fare and headed for a back seat. My eyes were clouded with unshed tears. I turned my face to the window. Had I been dishonest with myself? What did it really mean to be Aboriginal? I'd never lived off the land and been a hunter and a gatherer. I'd never participated in corroborees or heard stories of the Dreamtime.

I'd lived all my life in suburbia and told everyone I was Indian. I hardly knew any Aboriginal people. What did it mean for someone like me?

Halfway home, I felt so weighed down with all my questions that I decided to give it all up. I would telephone the department and tell them I wanted to go off the scholarship. My family would probably be relieved I wasn't trying to rock the boat any more. They could all go on being what they'd been for years, they wouldn't have to cope with a crazy member of the family who didn't know who she was. That's what I'd do. And I'd do it as soon as possible. I wasn't a brave person.

Just then, for some reason, I could see Nan. She was standing in front of me, looking at me. Her eyes were sad. 'Oh Nan,' I sighed, 'why did you have to turn up now, of all times?' She vanished as quickly as she'd come. I knew then that for some reason it was very important I stay on the scholarship. If I denied my tentative identification with the past now, I'd be denying her as well. I had to hold on to the fact that some day, it might all mean something.

When I told Jill about my interview, she was amazed. 'I'm glad it was you and not me,' she said. 'I couldn't have said what you did. I'd have let them think I was guilty. I can't stick up for myself like that.'

'I don't know how I did it, either,' I replied. 'But you know what? I'm really glad I did. From now on, I'm going to say more, be more assertive.'

'Heaven help us!'

On the weekend, I told Mum what had happened. She was much more upset than I had anticipated. She took it as a personal slight on herself.

Nan took an interest in the proceedings as well. She wasn't angry, just very pessimistic. 'You shouldn't have done it, Sally,' she growled. 'You don't know what they'll do now. They might send someone to the house. Government people are like that.'

'Oh don't be stupid, Nan,' Mum yelled. 'She did right to defend herself. No one's going to come snooping around.

Times have changed.'

'*You're* stupid, Glad.' Nan grunted, and before Mum could reply, she shuffled out to her bedroom.

'She's frightened,' Mum said. 'She's been frightened all her life. You can tell her things have changed, but she won't listen. She thinks it's still like the old days when people could do what they liked with you.'

'Could they, Mum?'

'Oh, I don't know. I don't want to talk now, Sally. Not now.'

However, my run-in with the Education Department did produce some unexpected results. Mum suddenly became more sympathetic to my desire to learn about the past. One day, she said to me, 'You know Nan was born on Corunna Downs Station, don't you?'

'I've heard her mention that station,' I replied, 'but whenever I've asked her about it, she clams up. Remember when David got that map of the north and showed her on the map where Corunna Downs was? She was quite excited. Yet she still won't talk.'

'I know. It really upsets me, sometimes.'

'Mum, who owned Corunna Downs?'

'Judy's father.'

'I didn't know that. What was his name?'

'Alfred Howden Drake-Brockman.'

'I suppose that's why Judy and Nan are so close.'

'Yes. Nan was Judy's nursemaid when she was little. She used to work very hard. Very, very hard...oh, I don't want to talk any more. Maybe some other time.'

For once, I accepted her decision without complaint. I knew now there would be other times.

I saw my family nearly every day. There were such strong bonds between us it was impossible for me not to want to see them. Just as well Paul was the uncomplaining sort!

One Saturday afternoon, I was over visiting Mum when she asked me to help her with Curly. 'He's in one of his cantankerous moods,' she said. 'He won't come inside.'

I eyed Curly from my standpoint on the front porch. He was lying in the middle of the road as usual. All morning, cars had been tooting at him. Curly moved for no one.

'You'll get run over, Curl,' I called in my Let's Be Reasonable voice. 'You'd better come in.' Still no response.

'You don't think he's going deaf in his old age?' Mum asked.

'Naah, just stupid.'

'He's a good dog, Sally,' she protested. 'You shouldn't talk about him like that.'

'I think you'd better go inside, Mum,' I advised. 'He'll never listen to me with you standing there.' Mum disappeared and I called once again to the flat layer of black fur lying on the road. 'Curl, Mum's gone now. If you don't come in, I'm gunna drag you in.' Curl raised his head slightly and growled. I knew what that meant. As soon as I touched him, he'd bite me. I'd been through this before.

'Listen, you bloody mongrel!' I yelled...

Before I could continue my tirade, Nan came up behind me and said, 'Don't say that, Sally, it hurts me here.' She patted her chest. 'Fancy my own granddaughter sayin' that. I never thought you'd be the one.'

'You're as bad as Mum,' I complained.

'I been called that,' Nan replied. 'It makes you feel real rotten inside.'

'It's no use you going on, Nan,' I said without listening, 'he *is* a mongrel!'

'Don't! Don't!' she said, as though I was inflicting some kind of pain on her.

'Nan,' I reasoned, 'someone has got to be firm with him or he'll get run over one day.'

'What are you talkin' about, Sally?'

'I'm talking about Curly,' I replied in exasperation, then paused. 'Why, what are you talking about?'

Nan gazed towards the oval directly opposite our house. Just where the bitumen ended and the grass began sat a small Aboriginal boy. I recognised him as belonging to a house around the corner from us.

'Nan!' I said in shock. 'You don't think I was calling that little fella a bloody mongrel, do you? Oh Nan, I'd never call a kid that. That's a terrible thing to call anyone. How could you think I'd do such a thing?'

'I've heard them called that. It's not right, they got feelings.'

'Nan, did you say you'd been called that?'

She put her hand over her mouth.

'Who was it, Nan?'

'Don't want to talk about it, Sally.'

'You've been called that more than once, haven't you, Nan?'

She ignored my question and turned to go inside. Half-way through the doorway, she stopped and said, 'Sal?'

'Yeah?'

'Promise me you won't ever call them that. When you see a little bloke like that, think of your Nanna.'

I nodded my head. I was too close to tears to reply. I wished I could wipe memories like that from her mind. She looked so vulnerable. It was times like this I realised just how much I loved her. Would she ever tell me the true story of my Aboriginal family? Maybe, one day...